Introductory Visual Basic

Introductory Visual Basic

2nd Edition

P.K. McBride

Continuum
London · New York

1997

Disclaimer

The programs presented in this book have been included for their instructional value. They have been tested with considerable care, but are not guaranteed for any particular purpose. The author and the publisher do not offer any warranties or representations, nor do they accept any liabilities with respect to the programs.

A CIP catalogue record for this book is available from the British Library

ISBN 0 8264 5386 4

Copyright © P.K. McBride 1994, 1997

First Edition 1994
Second Edition 1997
Reprinted 2000

 Typeset by P.K.McBride, Southampton

Printed in Great Britain by Ashford Colour Press Ltd, Gosport

Continuum
The Tower Building, 11 York Road, London, SE1 7NX
370 Lexington Avenue, New York, NY 10017-6550

Contents

Contents

Contents

Preface

Aim and need

Microsoft Windows is rapidly becoming the standard operating environment for PCs, and Visual Basic is the standard programming language for Windows. As a result, many employers are demanding that computing students are familiar with Visual Basic, and increasingly courses from National to degree level are including a Visual Basic component. This book has been specially written for these students, who are likely to have some programming experience and who need a concise and practical introductory-level text on Visual Basic.

Approach

This book assumes a basic knowledge of programming, using Pascal or Basic. It introduces the concepts and techniques of Visual Basic across a broad front. It then goes deeper into key aspects of the system, bringing in new objects and language elements as they are needed, and using larger (and more interesting) example programs for illustration. Appendix B gives a brief summary of the Visual Basic controls, listing their standard name prefix, main property and default event. The significance of each of these will become clear during the course of the book.

Where appropriate, there are short in-text programming tasks to enable students to practise immediately the techniques the text is introducing. These tasks do not require answers. At the end of most chapters, there are longer programming exercises, some of which have sample answers at the end of the book for student self-testing, and others of which have answers in the Lecturers' Supplement disk (see below for details).

Lecturers' Supplement

A free Lecturers' Supplement disk (3½ inch) is available to lecturers adopting this book as their course text, on application to the Publishers on college headed paper. Please state details of the course and likely student numbers. The disk contains suggested solutions to those questions for which there are no answers in the book.

Internet resources

The files for a selection of the programs developed in this book, including those that make heavy use of graphics, are available from the Visual Basic page on the author's World Wide Web site at:

    http://www.tcp.co.uk/~macbride

An Introduction to Visual Basic

Visual Basic is the language that many developers – including Microsoft themselves – are using to write new applications software. At the last count there were over a million Visual Basic applications in commercial use! Look closely at any modern Windows database, spreadsheet or word-processing package, whether from Microsoft or another leading software house, and you will find that its macro language is either a variety of Visual Basic, or almost identical to it. For this reason, anyone who wants to become a Windows 'expert' should master this language, and all Windows users, beyond the most casual, should have a grasp of it.

Visual Basic is substantially different from traditional Basics, though there are similarities. If you are already competent in Basic, it will be an advantage, and prior experience of programming in any language will help. Visual Basic requires a different approach to developing programs and to learning the language. In other Basics, you could develop a program line by line, testing each command as you write it. (It's not the most efficient way to write software, but it works.) You can take the same linear approach to learning the language, mastering one command at a time, and steadily building your knowledge. With Visual Basic you must develop your programs and your understanding across a broader front. You write a program by assembling the objects that you will use for screen displays and interaction with the users, adjusting the properties of those objects, determining which events you will respond to, thinking through the variables you need for holding data and for passing information from one part of the program to another, and writing the command lines that will run when events are activated. At each stage of development, you may add to or change any aspect of the program, but it must be done with an awareness of how it will affect the other aspects. Objects, properties, events and code are all interwoven. I have tried to take this same broad front approach in writing this book.

This second edition of *Introductory Visual Basic* has been written around Visual Basic 4.0, Standard edition but virtually all of the techniques and concepts apply equally well to earlier versions, and to Visual Basic 5.0. It does not attempt to cover the more advanced features or the development of free-standing commercial applications, for which the Professional Edition is essential. While there is a version of Visual Basic for DOS, it seems to be falling out of use and has been ignored in this book. Windows is the natural medium for Visual Basic.

P.K.McBride
August 1997

1 The Windows environment

1.1 Computer systems

Every computer system consists of three major elements – the hardware, applications software such as word-processors, spreadsheets, databases and language packages, and an operating system. The operating system is the element we tend to take for granted. It is composed of a core program, that controls the machine at its lowest level, and a set of tools for managing files and for configuring the machine to the user's own requirements.

DOS

In a PC, the operating system is MS-DOS. This was developed for IBM by Microsoft, modelled on CP/M. This Control Program for Microprocessors was designed by Gary Kildall for the earlier personal computers and was the most successful O/S (Operating System) in use at that time. Like CP/M, and unlike earlier operating systems, MS-DOS is not limited to one type of hardware. Its core program – the BIOS (Basic Input Output System) – is split into two portions. Part is machine-specific and contains the routines that send data along or collect it from the wires to the screen, keyboard, disk drive and other peripherals; the other part provides fixed points of entry for the applications software.When a program wants to print a character on the screen, for instance, it passes that character to the appropriate routine in the upper BIOS, which passes it to the machine-specific part and on to the hardware.

The beauty of this approach is that it enables the same programs to be run on any hardware, as long as it has MS-DOS, and to make MS-DOS suitable for a new computer, it is only necessary to modify the machine-specific portion. For reasons best known to IBM and Microsoft, Microsoft has retained control of the copyright and can license MS-DOS to other computer manufacturers. These are then able to produce 'IBM-compatible' machines – usually cheaper and often better than the real thing. MS-DOS has been hugely successful and has dominated business and personal computing since the mid-80s.

Windows

Microsoft has not stood still. They have produced a steady stream of new versions, to accommodate advances in hardware and to offer new facilities to the user. They have also developed Windows. This now exists in three main versions – Windows 95 is the one normally installed on new PCs; Windows NT is the common choice for networked offices; and Windows 3.1, the final revision of the original system, is still widely used. Yet another new version, Windows 98, is promised for 1998.

Windows is not an operating system, it is a GUI – Graphical User Interface. It was not an original concept, but a response to the GUI machines so successfully marketed by Apple. A GUI acts as a friendly 'front-end' making it easier for you to interact with the computer. There are three main aspects to this. First, instead of typing command lines, you can carry out operations by pointing at icons on the screen, or selecting from menus – and this greatly reduces the amount you have to learn and remember. Secondly, it allows you to have several programs running at once, each in its own

1

'window'. While you cannot do two jobs simultaneously, you can switch rapidly between them and transfer data easily from one to another. The third aspect is that all applications designed to run under Windows have a common appearance and work in similar ways, so that once you have learnt to use one, subsequent progams are easier to learn.

MS-DOS is still there, running beneath Windows and providing the low-level control of the hardware, but this is irrelevant to us as Visual Basic programmers. What is relevant is that your access to the screen, the keyboard, the disk drives, the mouse and all the rest of the hardware, is via Windows. The result is to make most things easier to perform, but also to set some restrictions on what you can do.

1.2 Hardware

For a PC to be able to run Windows 3.1, it must have an 80386 or later processor, at least 2 Megabytes of RAM memory, a 40 Megabyte hard disk and an EGA screen display.

Windows 95 and NT require a higher specification – an 80486 or Pentium processor, at least 8 Megabytes of RAM, a 200+ Megabytes hard disk and a VGA screen.

These are very much the minimums. Windows is a graphical system and, like all such systems, requires a lot of processor power and memory if it is to operate efficiently. A large hard disk is generally needed, for Windows applications are normally very hungry for disk space. Visual Basic itself will take around 12 Mb of storage, and even a small Visual Basic program will occupy around 50Kb. (On a network, where applications software may all be stored centrally on a file-server, each machine should have its own hard disk so that it can have its own copy of Windows, if running speeds are not to suffer.) While an EGA or a monochrome VGA screen display will do, Windows programs are written for, and look best on, high-resolution colour screens.

Realistic hardware platforms are:

	Windows 3.1	Windows 95/NT
Processor	80386 or 80486	Pentium 166
RAM memory	4 to 8 Mb	16Mb
Hard disk	80Mb or more	400Mb
Monitor	VGA colour	SVGA colour

1.3 Windows, icons and menus

The Visual Basic system runs within Windows and produces programs that can only run within Windows. It follows that you must be happy about working within the Windows environment before you attempt to start working with Visual Basic. If you are completely new to Windows, I would suggest that you spend an hour or two exploring that system first. Play the games, draw some pictures with Paintbrush (Paint on Windows 95), root around the directories with the File Manager (Explorer on Windows 95) and dip into the Help pages wherever you go. You don't need to become an expert, but you should at least learn these basic techniques.

Control the mouse

- **Click** the **left** button to locate the cursor, select options or highlight items.
- **Double-click** (press twice rapidly) to load files, and sometimes to select operations. In general, if a single click doesn't do the job, try a double.
- **Drag** – hold down the left button and move the mouse – to move things around the screen, highlight areas or change the size of objects.
- Point to an object and click the **right** mouse button to open a short menu of common commands that can be used with that object.

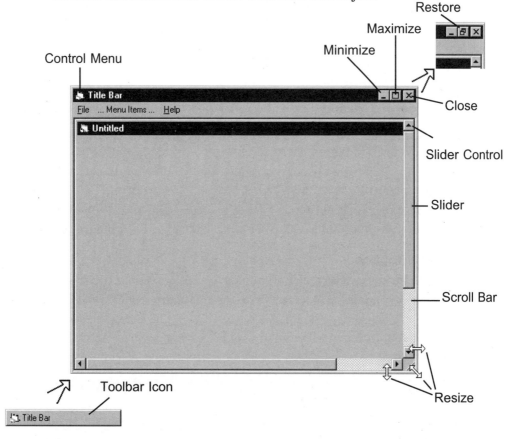

Figure 1.1 A Window and its Control Buttons (Windows 95).

Use the window frame

- **Move** the window by dragging on the title bar.
- **Resize** it by dragging on the edge or corner of the frame.
- **Scroll** the view through the window using the scroll bar – either by clicking the arrows or dragging the slider.
- Call up the **Control Menu** by clicking the top left icon.
- **Close** a window by clicking the top right button. (Windows 95)
- **Close** a window by double-clicking the top left icon. (Windows 3.1)
- Click the **Maximize** button to switch to full screen.

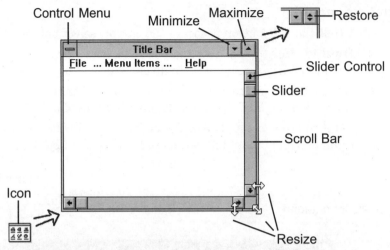

Figure 1.2 A Window and its Control Buttons (Windows 3.1).

- Click the **Restore** button (the double-headed arrow) to shrink a full screen window back to normal size.
- Click the **Minimize** button to reduce the window to an icon on the Toolbar (normally – and best – kept at the bottom of the screen).
- **Click** a Toolbar icon to restore it to a normal window. (Windows 95)
- **Double-click** a Minimized icon to restore the normal window. (Windows 3.1)

Good working practice

- Try to keep the screen tidy. It will save a lot of trouble.
- Avoid overlapping windows by reducing unwanted ones to icons.
- If you do want several windows open at once, adjust the size of each so that they are no larger than necessary, and arrange them so that each is clearly visible and accessible.

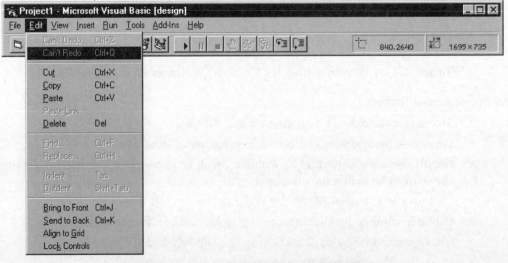

Figure 1.3 A Typical Menu Display.

Select from menus

- Those options that are applicable at the time are shown in bold – others are 'greyed-out'. **To make a selection**, move the highlight bar to an option by dragging it, or by pointing and clicking.

- **To abandon a menu** without making a selection, point and click elsewhere on the screen.

- If you prefer to **use the keyboard**, open menus from the top bar by holding **[Alt]** and pressing the underlined initial of the one you want, e.g. Alt-F will open the File menu. Once into the menu system, an option can be selected by pressing the underlined letter – these are not necessarily the initial.

- Some commands have a **keystroke shortcut** which allows you to bypass the menu system, e.g. Ctrl-X has the same effect as the menu sequence **Edit | Cut**.

As with much of the latest Windows software, a few of the most commonly used commands have icon equivalents. We will look at these in the next section.

Get out of trouble

Windows can be confusing. One careless click and the window you are working on can disappear beneath another. If you lose track of what is happening, try this.

- Hold **[Alt]** and press the **[Tab]** key to make the **Task selector** appear.

- Keep **[Alt]** down and press **[Tab]** to move the highlight box onto the icon for the application you want and use.

- Release **[Alt]** to switch to the selected application.

If all else fails, and you really cannot see what is happening to your system or nothing seems to be happening at all, hold down [Ctrl] and [Alt] and press [Delete]. That will open a dialog box called Close Program in Windows 95, and Task List in Windows 3.1.

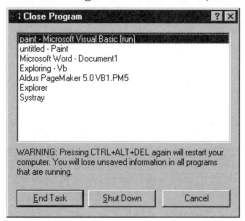

Figure 1.4 The Close Program dialog box (Windows 95).

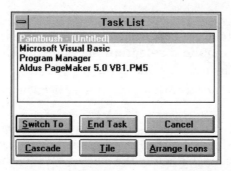

Figure 1.5 The Task List (Windows 3.1).

If Windows is struggling, the program or application at the top of the list is most likely to be the cause of the trouble. Select it and click **End Task**.

Task 1.1   If you have not already done so, familiarise yourself with Windows. Learn how to open and close windows, switch between applications, and use the Explorer (Windows 95) or File Manager (Windows 3.1).

Windows 95 and 3.1

For the rest of the book, all the illustrations are taken from Windows 95 screens. If you are working inWindows 3.1, you will notice a few minor – and irrelevant – differences. All the essential parts of the system and the display are the same whatever version of Windows you are using.

2 Visual Basic concepts

2.1 Event-driven programming

Traditional programming is essentially linear and based on the flow of execution. Operations run for a fixed span or until they reach decision points written into the program, and interrupting an on-going activity is either difficult or impossible to manage. Programmers are responsible for all aspects of their program, including the screen display and user interface, and must write the code to do everything. If they want particularly elegant screen effects, then they have got their work cut out. Programs are usually designed from top down, perhaps following the Jackson Structured Programming method, by decomposing complex operations into successively simpler ones. Sometimes a modular approach will be taken, creating a program from a set of more-or-less self-contained functions and procedures. In theory this makes it possible to reuse modules – perhaps those that produce the fancy screen effects – in other programs. In practice, there are generally very few routines that can be reused without major reworking.

Object-oriented programming

Visual Basic is *object oriented*, i.e it revolves around ready-made objects, and it is *event driven*, i.e all the activities in a program are triggered by one event or another. Each object has its own *properties*, determining its position, size, colour, the appearance and nature of its text, and much more. Each object also has its own *event-handling procedures*. The Visual Basic system knows all about these already. It knows what a button is and how it works. It also knows how to handle images, menus, dialog boxes, drive and directory lists, and much else.

The programmer's job is to determine where, how and when an object appears on screen, what its caption reads, and what happens when an event occurs. That event might be the opening of a form, the user clicking on a button or typing text into a box. The programmer does not have to write code to trap these events – the system does that automatically. Because the program code runs in response to events, and as at any point a whole range of events might be possible, the flow of execution is not as fixed as in a traditional program. Operations do not have to follow a set sequence and can be easily interrupted, suspended or abandoned.

The process of program design reflects the nature of the system. You begin by creating the screen layout (the user-interface in the jargon), and work outwards from here, adding first the code that will run in response to specific events and then any necessary code to co-ordinate the whole program.

Task 2.1   Compare some DOS-based software with its Windows equivalent – either a word processor or a language compiler would be a good example. How much easier is it to learn and use the Windows package? What part does the presence of an interactive graphical screen play in this ease of use?

2.2 Terminology

Form

The form is the central unit in Visual Basic. It is a window, initially blank, on which you paste *controls* (see below) to create your screen or printer display. The form can be any size or colour, and you can attach to it code that will run when the form is loaded, closed or when the mouse is clicked or moves over it. A simple program may use only one form, others may have several forms, each of which will handle a different part of the program. One form may be for getting input from the user, a second for displaying results on the screen, a third for sending output to the printer. Each form is saved on disk as a separate file, with a .FRM extension.

Controls

These are the objects which can be pasted onto a form and range from labels which display text, through picture boxes for graphic images, to buttons, check boxes, lists and other menus, to file management utilities and spreadsheet-style grids. Their properties, and the events they can handle, vary to suit their nature. Each control can have code attached to it – though not all will have. A text label or a graphic image, for example, may well be there simply to improve the display, and not as the startpoint for any activities.

Module

Code that is attached to a form is accessible from anywhere on that form, but a program may have more than one form. It will sometimes be necessary to have program code that can be reached from any form, and in this case the code would be written on a module. Modules disappear from view when the program runs – only forms have an on-screen existence. There may be several modules in one program, and each is saved as a separate file. These are marked by a .BAS extension.

Project

The project holds together the various forms and modules that make up a program. Its purpose is primarily one of convenience. When you want to start work on a program, you only have to open the one project file – marked by a .MAK extension – rather than a whole set of forms and modules.

Procedure

All the code in a program is written in procedures, or subroutines. Most of these will be attached to a control – or more accurately to an event belonging to a control. Some will be free-standing. All start with the keyword **Sub** and close with **End Sub**.

2.3 The working screen

When you load up Visual Basic, the initial screen will look something like that shown in Figure 2.1. Note that there is no single Visual Basic window. Instead, each part of the system is displayed in its own window and each part can be moved, re-sized, or tucked out of view. This has several implications. First, and least important, is that your screen is unlikely to look exactly the same as the screenshots in this book. Secondly, you can tailor your screen to suit your own way of working. Last – and a possible cause of error – is that the windows of any other open applications will be partially visible in the gaps between the Visual Basic windows, and clicking on one will bring it to the front. If you find that you keep doing this by mistake, minimise the other windows to icons, so that they are out of the way.

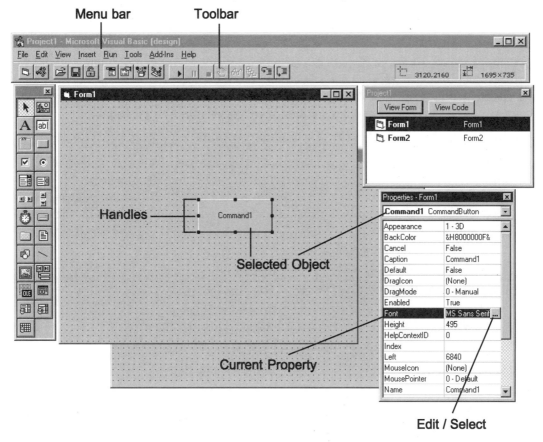

Figure 2.1 The Visual Basic desktop, showing the main component windows.

The Menu bar and the Toolbar

The top window gives access to the commands that are used at the design stage. Many of the commands in the Menu system have keyboard shortcuts, and the most commonly used ones also have icon equivalents. The menu structure is well organised, with commands almost always where you would expect them to be. We will take a brief tour of the menus in Section 2.5 to see the range of commands on offer.

Task 2.2   Get Visual Basic up and running. Identify the component windows and arrange them so that each is clearly visible. If any are not present, open them using the options on the View menu (see page 16).

The Project window

This is used for moving between forms and modules, and between Form and Code Views. If the program only has one Form, this serves little purpose and can be allowed to disappear beneath other windows.

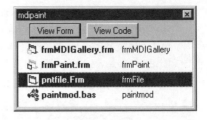

The Form window

This is the blank sheet on which you will assemble your screen display, using the controls. It is possible, but not usually practical, to create a display by using commands to write and draw directly on the form. The form can act as a normal, movable and resizable window, or can have a fixed size and position.

2.4 The Toolbox

This fixed-size but movable window holds the controls. What is surprising, and gratifying, is not just the range of the facilities on offer, but also the depth of the work that some of them do. As you read through the list, think how much code you would have to write to create equivalent facilities if you were using a traditional programming language.

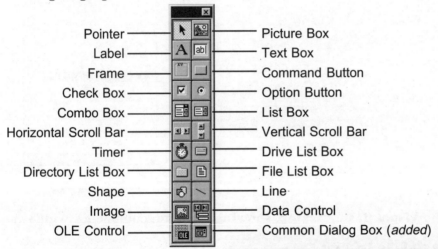

Figure 2.2 The Controls.

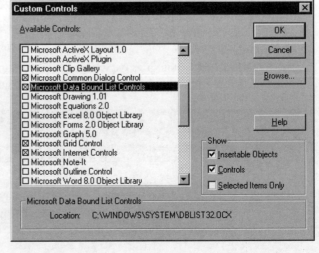

Initially, the Toolbox contains only the standard Visual Basic controls, but icons for other controls and objects can be added. (The Common Dialog control – see Chapter 15 – has been added to the Toolbox shown above.)

To add more controls, right click on the Toolbox for its menu and select Custom Controls, then tick the checkboxes for the ones you want.

The **Pointer** is different from the rest of the tools, and is used for selecting objects that have been placed on the form. The system reverts to this when you have finished using any other tool. It is marked by an arrow cursor.

All the control tools are used in a similar way. When one is selected, a crosshair cursor appears. Place this on the form and drag to create an outline where the control is to go. It does not matter if you get the initial position or size wrong, as it can be adjusted later with the Pointer.

A **Picture Box** is the main graphics control. It can hold pictures created with Paint or similar art packages. These must be in an acceptable format – .BMP, .WMF, .ICO or .DIB, but not .PCX. The drawing methods (see Chapter 7) can also be used in a Picture box.

Labels and **Text Box**es both hold text, but only the Text Box is capable of receiving input from the user. So, use Labels for your messages and prompts, and Text Boxes for replies.

A **Frame** simply holds things together. If you place a set of controls within a frame, they are all moved together as the frame is moved. Note that once a control has been placed in a frame, it cannot be moved out onto the form, and vice versa.

Command Buttons are one method of selection. They are typically used where there are only a limited number of options – the choice may be OK or Cancel, Start or Quit.

Check Boxes act as toggle switches, turning options on or off.

Option Buttons are normally used to select one from a set of mutually exclusive options. At any one time there can only be one set on a form, unless they are enclosed in frames.

List Boxes display lists of items, so that the user can see what is available and select one. If the list is too long to fit in the box, vertical scroll bars will be added at runtime. Items can only be added to the list during runtime, not at design time

A **Combo Box** combines a drop-down list with a slot in which users can enter their own data when the program is running.

The **Horizontal** and **Vertical Scroll Bar**s are used on forms to give a very flexible means of setting values. You set the minimum and maximum values – anything between -32768 and 32767. When the program is running, the position of the slider determines the value returned by the scroll bar.

The **Timer** is unusual in that it is of fixed size and is invisible once the program is running. Its purpose is to control actions that must take place at or after set intervals. You could use one to set a time limit for a response to a question, to produce a ticking clock or to animate images.

The **Drive List box**, **Directory List box** and **File List box** can be used together to give the standard Windows file management facilities. When the program runs they will initially display the current drive and directory. These can be changed by clicking and highlighting in the usual way. It takes a minimum amount of programming to link the three boxes together and produce a highly efficient file selection routine.

The **Shape** (either a circle, oval, square or rectangle) and the **Line** are for purely decorative purposes. For anything other than the simplest design, you will probably be better off creating it with Paintbrush and importing into a picture or image box.

An **Image** is a simple container for displaying BMP, ICO or DIB pictures. It has far fewer features than a Picture box, but is updated faster.

OLE stands for Object Linking and Embedding. This control allows you to make a two-way link with an object in another Windows application. The data in the object can then be edited in either your program or in the original application – there is only the one object. This is a memory-hungry activity and is not possible on all machines.

The **Common Dialog** control is an optional extra, added through the Custom Controls routine. It produces standard Windows 3.1 dialog boxes for file opening and saving, printing and similar operations.

Task 2.3 Use the Toolbox to place some controls on your form. Make sure that you include a Label and a Command Button, as these will be wanted later in this section. Delete everything but the Label and the Button by first clicking on them, then pressing [Delete]. Adjust the size and position of your two objects with the Pointer, so that you have a layout something like that in Figure 2.3.

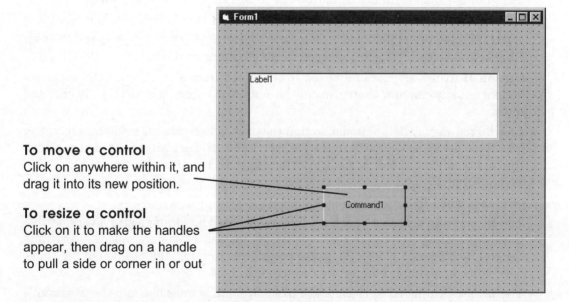

To move a control
Click on anywhere within it, and drag it into its new position.

To resize a control
Click on it to make the handles appear, then drag on a handle to pull a side or corner in or out

Figure 2.3 The first job in creating a program is to put controls on the form.

2.5 The Properties window

This is where you set the properties of objects. To do this:

- Click on the **object**, or select its name from the drop-down list at the top of this window.
- Select the **property** to be set from the list.

The range of properties varies with the nature of the object, but always covers its visible features and some aspects of its interaction with the rest of the system.

The properties list for a Label, shown here, includes:

- **Caption** – the text that is written inside it;
- **Font** specifications – Size, Name, Bold, Italic, other styles and Alignment;
- **Color** controls – for the Forecolor and the BackColor;
- **Name** – edit this to change the default names of Label1, Label2, and the like, to something meaningful. There is little point in doing that here, but as programs get more complex, memorable names become more useful.

The text for the Caption and Name can be edited with the normal Windows editing techniques.

The **new value** can be typed directly into the Edit slot, or chosen from a set of options. Most of these are given in *drop-down lists*, indicated by a ▾. Some of these lists are simply a choice of *True* or *False* to turn an effect on or off; others are more extensive.

Fonts are set and picture files selected through *dialog boxes*, both indicated by ⃞.

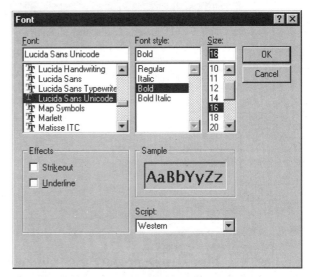

In Visual Basic, you have the same range of Fonts as elsewhere in your Windows system. The size, style and special effects can be set from here – use the Sample box to see how the settings will look.

If you want to change the colour, set the ForeColor property.

Note that new values can be assigned to properties within a program, as you will see below in *Attaching Code* (page 20).

Task 2.4	Explore the properties of the form and of the controls on your screen.
	Change the Label's Caption to "Pressure Tester";
	Font Size, from the drop-down list, to 18;
	Fore and Back Colors, to any other colours.
	Change the Button's Caption to read "Click".

2.6 The Color palette

This is not normally visible, but can be turned on from the View menu (see page 16). To set colours with this, first select the control, then click in the centre (ForeColor) or outside (BackColor) of the square on the left, and then click on the desired colour.

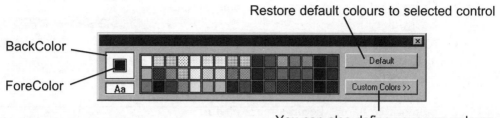

Restore default colours to selected control

BackColor

ForeColor

You can also define your own colours

Figure 2.4 The Color Palette.

2.7 Controls and events

Just as each type of control has its own set of properties, some of which are common to all, so each also has its own set of events, and some of these are common to all. To see what kind of events are handled, place an object on the form and double-click on it. This opens the **code window**. It is here that you write the code to be attached to events.

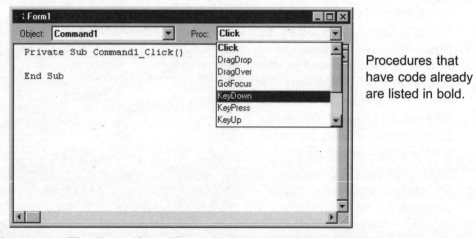

Procedures that have code already are listed in bold.

Figure 2.5 The Procedure list pulled down within a code window.

Each event has its own procedure, or **Sub**, and the opening and closing lines of these are already written for you. The name, in the opening line, is composed of the names of the control and the event, linked by an underscore. **Private** at the start means that the code can only be accessed from that control or other controls on the same form. If you wanted to open up the code so that it could be read from other forms – unlikely until you get much further into Visual Basic – this should be changed to **Public**.

There is always a set of ( ) brackets at the end of the name. Some of these will be empty, but with some events there will be variable names in the brackets. These are used to carry information from the event through to your code. With a Text box's Keypress event, for example, the opening line of the procedure reads:

Private Sub Text1_KeyPress (KeyAscii As Integer)

When this event is triggered, *KeyAscii* will hold the Ascii code of the key that was pressed. The code might well check this to see if the user had pressed a specific key, or one from an acceptable range.

When the code window first opens, it will display the procedure for the most commonly used event for that type of control. For example, with a Command button, you are always offered the Click event. If this is not the event you want to handle, then you can select another by dropping down the **Proc:** list. If an event is not in that list, then the control cannot respond to it.

Task 2.5 Explore the event of the controls on your form. Which ones crop up regularly? Which ones are specific to certain controls?

2.8 The menu system

The File menu

A Visual Basic program consists of a Project containing one or more Forms and Modules. These are both *Files* and there are options to Save, Add or Remove them independently. Most commands lead on to a standard Windows dialog box, where you can set the drive and directory, and either select a file or specify a name.

At the bottom of the menu are a set of .Vbp filenames, representing the last four programs that were worked on. Clicking on a name here opens the project – a quicker alternative to using **File | Open Project** and the dialog box.

There are icons for two of the **File** commands.

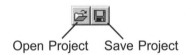

Open Project   Save Project

The Edit menu

The **Undo** and **Redo** commands change as you work, and are only available when actions can be undone or redone.

The usual Clipboard set – **Cut, Copy** and **Paste** – are present, to allow you to copy or move data from one place to another. You will find these particularly useful for reorganising your program code, both within and between procedures. They can also be put to good use duplicating controls when you are designing a complex form.

Find and **Replace** are active when you are editing code. Use them to track down or rename variables.

Indent and **Outdent** are used for tidying up the layout of your code – **[Tab]** and **[Shift]+[Tab]** do exactly the same, quicker!

File	
New Project	
Open Project...	Ctrl+O
Save File	Ctrl+S
Save File As...	Ctrl+A
Save Project	
Save Project As...	
Add File...	Ctrl+D
Remove File	
Print Setup...	
Print...	Ctrl+P
Make EXE File...	
1 C:\PM5\VB\files\mines.Vbp	
2 C:\PM5\VB\files\mdipaint.vbp	
3 C:\PM5\VB\files\rand.vbp	
4 C:\PM5\VB\files\walkman.Vbp	
Exit	

Edit	
Can't Undo	Ctrl+Z
Can't Redo	Ctrl+Q
Cut	Ctrl+X
Copy	Ctrl+C
Paste	Ctrl+V
Paste Link	
Delete	Del
Find...	Ctrl+F
Replace...	Ctrl+H
Indent	Tab
Outdent	Shift+Tab
Bring to Front	Ctrl+J
Send to Back	Ctrl+K
Align to Grid	
Lock Controls	

The bottom set are active when you are working with objects on a form. Use these to control the overlapping of objects and as an aid to accurate positioning.

Lock Controls 🔒 should be applied when you have got everything positioned just so – it stops you from moving anything by accident.

The View menu

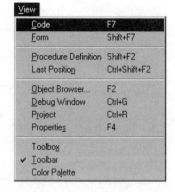

The options on this menu are used for browsing through your code and for opening the various windows that make up the Visual Basic system.

Code and **Form** apply to the currently selected form, and switch you between the Code window and the Form design. These and their key equivalents ([F7] for Code, [Shift]+[F7] for Form) are particularly useful when working with large windows.

When you are in the Code window, **Procedure Definition** will locate the code for a selected procedure, and **Last Position** will step you back through the moves you have made through your code.

Which windows can be opened at any time depends upon what you are doing. **Project, Properties, Toolbox** and **Toolbar** are opened automatically when you are designing a form. If for any reason they are not visible now, select their names now to open them. You may also want to open the **Color Palette** at this stage.

The Debug Window is used at runtime, to trace the values held by variables or properties. (See Chapter 6.)

The **Object Browser** lists the methods and properties in the classes and modules of your project – and also in the Visual Basic system. Use it to remind yourself of what is available and what the ready-made methods do, and to look at the procedures that you have written.

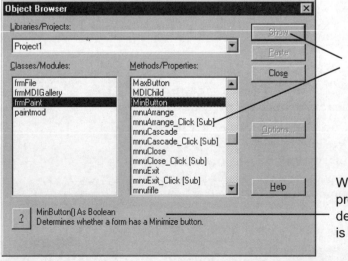

Procedures that you have written are marked (Sub). Select one and click Show to see its code.

With ready-made methods and properties, a definition and brief description of the selected one is shown here.

Figure 2.6 The Object Browser.

Three View commands have icon equivalents: **Project, Object Browser** and **Properties**. Of these, **Properties** is a handy way to pull the Property window to the front of the display, should it have become hidden beneath a mass of forms – it happens!

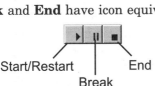

Properties | Project
Object Browser

The Insert menu

This is used for adding new elements to your project. The two which you will use most often – Form and Module – are also present as Toolbar icons.

Insert new Form   Insert new Module

The Run menu

Start will set your programs running. **Start with Full Compile** will also execute them, but in trying to compile first, it will pick up some errors that would only otherwise show up during execution (see Chapter 6).

Once a program is running, **Start** is replaced by **Break**, which halts program execution so that you can look closer at what's happening. **End** and **Restart** (after a Break) are active only at run-time.

The **Step** and **Breakpoint** options are used for working through a program in stages, to find errors. See Chapter 6 for more on these, and other aspects of debugging.

Run, Break and **End** have icon equivalents.

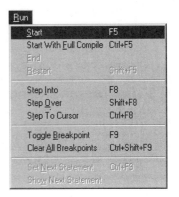

Start/Restart | End
Break

The Tools menu

This menu has an odd mixture on it. The **Watch** and **Calls** options are used in debugging, and might have been better put on the **Run** menu.

The **Menu Editor** is for creating and editing menus within programs.

Custom Controls... opens the dialog box we met earlier, when looking at the Toolbox (page 10).

References are for experts. Ignore them.

Options... allows you to configure the way your Visual Basic system works. We will be looking at a few of them later, but all are best left at the Default settings until you have much more experience of the system.

The Add-Ins menu

The **Data Manager** is an extension package that gives Visual Basic the ability to can read Access, dBase, Paradox and other standard database files.

The **Add-in Manager** lets you link other extension packages, from Microsoft or other developers, into Visual Basic. You may well have nothing suitable on your system.

The Help menu

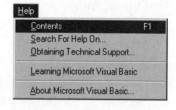

The Help system is well organised and very comprehensive. Choose the **Search** if you know exactly what you are after, or the **Contents** option for a topic-based approach. Within the Contents, the **Programming Language** section takes you to an indexed list of all aspects of the language, while Objects leads on to details of the Controls, their properties and events. Use this well. It is packed with detailed information, and has many practical examples. **Learning Microsoft Visual Basic** runs an introductory tutorial, that is also well worth a look.

Context-sensitive Help is also available from the **F1** key. When you press this, the system will display a page of help relating to the currently selected object on a form layout, or to a highlighted word in your code. Try it as you explore the screen.

2.9 The programming language

Some words in the Visual Basic vocabulary will be familiar to those who have programmed in other Basics; others arise from the Windows environment. One of the noticeable features of the language is that it has a large vocabulary – something around 1,000 words! If you want to know what is there, open the **Help** menu, select **Contents** and then **Programming Language**. This will present you with a full alphabetical list of the vocabulary. Fortunately you do not have to learn them all. It is enough to know what is available, in general terms, as you can look up the exact word and its mode of use in the Help pages. The language divides into three categories.

Statements

These are words that do things. Some you may well recognise from other Basics. For example:

ChDir D:\files\mydata

which **Ch**anges the **Dir**ectory.

For n = 1 To 10
...
Next n

where the key words are **For ... To ... Next** that cause a set of commands to be executed a set number of times.

Others will be quite new. For instance:

MsgBox "Welcome to this program"

MsgBox generates a standard Windows message box with the usual OK button. The text can be whatever you like – in this case it will display "Welcome to this program".

Functions

These take numbers, strings of text or other forms of data, perform an operation upon them and return a new value to the program. For example:

wordlen = Len(inputword)

Here **Len** calculates the length of the text in the variable *inputword*. If this had held "Dictionary", the resulting value of 10 would be passed back to the variable *wordlen*.

Many of the functions will be familiar to those of you who have used traditional Basics, but – as with Statements – some are specific to this system.

surname = InputBox ("Please enter your name")

InputBox, like MsgBox, arises from Windows. This displays a standard dialog box, with your prompt, the usual *OK* and *Cancel* buttons, and a slot in which to type data.

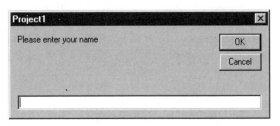

In this example, whatever is typed into the dialog box is copied across to the variable *surname*. The function is used here in its simplest form. With very little extra effort you can add a title to the box, or a big bright **?** or **!** symbol, or replace the *OK* with *Yes* and *No* buttons.

Methods

These are not found in traditional Basics, though their names, and what they do may be familiar. Like statements, they perform actions, but these can only be used with suitable objects. e.g.:

Picture1.Circle (x,y) radius
Form1.Print "Hello Mum"

The first draws a circle in the control called *Picture1*; the second prints a greeting on *Form1*. You can only print on objects that can handle text, or draw circles in those that can handle graphics. Different types of objects have different sets of methods that can be used with them.

The syntax

This is the set of rules that govern how command lines must be written. The syntax for any given command can be found in the Help pages, and shows the keywords, the essential and the optional parameters, and the punctuation. It is written following certain conventions.

- Items in **bold** are reserved words – these appear in blue in the completed line.
- Items in *italics* are parameters. They may be the names of objects or variables, number or string values, or expressions which produce numbers or strings. Those enclosed by [square brackets] are optional. The others are essential.

For example, the syntax for **Circle** Method reads:

[*object.*]Circle [Step](*x,y*),*radius* [,[*color*] [,[*start*] [,[*end*] [,*aspect*]]]]

This shows that an *object* name is optional – it is not needed if the method is part of a routine attached to the object; **Step** is an optional keyword that modifies the way the method works; in the parameters, *x, y* and *radius* are all essential; *color, start, end* and *aspect* are all optional. The effect of the options and the type of values wanted for the parameters are all detailed further down the Help page.

Task 2.6 Call up the Help system and look up each of the keywords covered above. What do the Syntax lines tell you about the way each command is used?

2.10 Attaching code

Where code is to be executed in response to an event, it is written into the code window of the object that handles the event. If you did Task 2.3, you should have a form containing a Label and a Command button. That button can handle, amongst other events, one called **Click**. We will add a little code so that when the button is clicked, three messages appear on the screen. Each will be produced by a different type of code.

Double click on the button control. A window will open, containing two lines of code:

```
Private Sub Command1_Click ( )
|
End Sub
```

You will notice that **Private, Sub**, **End Sub** and the (brackets) are in blue. (This is the default, but it depends upon your setup.) Reserved words and symbols, which have a special meaning to the system, are shown in a different colour from other text. The cursor is waiting in the space between these lines.

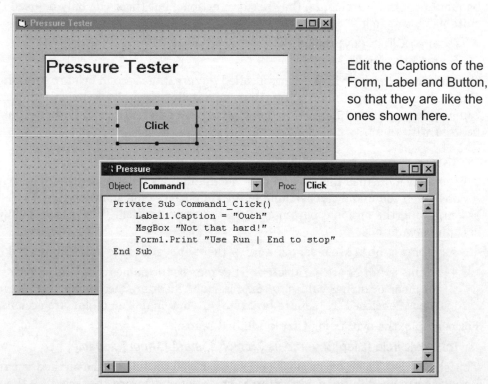

Edit the Captions of the Form, Label and Button, so that they are like the ones shown here.

Figure 2.7 The Form and the code window for the command button.

Type in the following – and don't worry about capitals – the system will add these when it checks the lines, but do note that there are no spaces within **Label1.Caption**, or **Form1.Print**:

```
Label1.Caption = "Ouch"
MsgBox "Not that hard!"
Form1.Print "Use Run | End to stop"
```

- The first line is an example of changing the value of a property within a program. It assigns the text "Ouch" to the Caption property of the Label.
- The second uses the **MsgBox** statement.
- The third uses the **Print** method to display a message directly on the form.

Run the program, by selecting **Run | Start** or clicking the icon. Click the button and see what happens. Click it as often as you like. The code will continue to respond to the event as long as the program is running.

To end the program, select **Run | End** from the menu or use the icon or press **[Ctrl]** and **[Break]**.

To save the program for posterity, turn to the **File** menu.

- First select **Save File As**, to save the form. Use the dialog box to get to the directory where you will store your Basic files and give it a suitable name.
- Next select **Save Project As**. The path will be pointing to the right directory already, so all you need do is type in a name.

2.11 Variables

As with other Basics, you do not have to declare variables before you first use them, though your code is always easier to read – and often easier to write – if you do. Declaration is done with the **Dim** statement, followed by the variable's name and type.

The rules for **variable names** are simple:

- they must begin with a letter;
- they may contain any mixture of letters and numbers;
- they may not include punctuation or symbols, with the exception of the under_score;
- they may not have more than 40 characters.

If you make the names meaningful, your code will be easier for you and others to read, and if you keep them short, you will reduce typing mistakes;

Visual Basic supports a wider range of **variable types** than is found in other Basics.

Integer	whole numbers in the range –32,768 to +32,767;
Long	whole numbers in the range + or – 2 billion;
Single	floating point numbers (i.e. very large or with decimal fractions) held accurately to 7 digits;
Double	as Single, but held to 15 digit accuracy;
Currency	numbers in the range + or – 900,000 billion, held to 19-digit accuracy;
String	text with up to 65,000 characters;

Variant   a highly flexible form of storage that can take String or number values. The nature of the variable can change during the program's run, so that at one point it may take in a String value, but later treat it as a number – perhaps in a calculation. If you do not specify a type, variables are treated as Variants.

It is also possible to define your own types of variables (see Chapter 12).

Examples of variable declarations:

     Dim Num1 As Integer

     Dim Salary As Currency

     Dim Surname As String   (See Note 1)

     Dim x As Integer, y As Integer   (See Note 2)

Notes: 1. You do not need a dollar sign ($) at the end of a String variable name, as you do in most Basics.

          2. You can have several variables in a Dim line, but each must be typed unless you want them to be Variants.

2.12 Arrays

Variable arrays can be huge. An array may have up to 60 dimensions, and a dimension may have up to 32,767 subscripts. However, this does not mean that you can have 60 dimension, each with 32,767 subscripts – you will run out of memory long before this. The practical maximum number of elements in an array is around 1 million – depending upon the type of variable and the capacity of your machine. Note that subscript numbering starts from 0 unless you specify otherwise.

Arrays should be declared with **Dim** in the general declarations area, or with **Redim** (see below) in a procedure.

Examples of array declarations:

     Dim Results(50) As Integer

This creates a one-dimensional array of 51 integers, numbered from 0 to 50.

     Dim Employees(1..200) As String

This will hold 200 text items, each of any length up to 64K. In this case the subscript numbering starts at 1.

     Dim Table(10,20) As Single

This array has two dimensions, which you could think of as 10 columns and 20 rows.

     Dim OxoGrid(3,3,3) As Integer

The last could be the 'playing area' for a game of three-dimensional Noughts and Crosses, with 4 layers of 4 rows and 4 columns.

In Visual Basic you can also have **control arrays** – sets of identical controls that, like variable names, have a common name and identifying numbers. (See Chapter 9.)

2.13 Scope and duration of variables

A variable's scope – the code within which it can be accessed – is normally restricted to the procedure or module in which it was written. A variable declared with a **Dim** in a procedure exists only within that procedure and its value is lost when the procedure ends. One declared within the special **declarations** procedure of a form can be read or changed from anywhere within that form, but not from other forms in the program.

Even though you may not want to use any of these during the early stages of your programming, it is worth knowing that there are alternatives to **Dim**, as sometimes they can provide a neater solution to a problem.

Static

Use this instead of **Dim** in a procedure if you want the variable to retain its value when the procedure ends. For example, you might have this code attached to a command button called *cmdAdd*:

```
Sub cmdAdd_Click()
    Static TotalSoFar As Integer
    TotalSoFar = TotalSoFar + NextNumber
End Sub
```

If *TotalSoFar* had been set up with **Dim**, its value would have been reset to zero every time the button was clicked. Using **Static**, we can keep a running total in *TotalSoFar*, adding to it each time *cmdAdd* is clicked.

Global

Where you have a separate Basic module – i.e. free-standing code – variables declared with **Global** are accessible from any form within the program.

ReDim

Use this to set up arrays if you want to be able to change their size during the execution of the program – the size might depend on how much data the user wanted to store. **Redim** is an active command, to be used in a procedure or module, not in the *general declarations* area. Existing data is normally erased from the array. Example:

```
Redim Marks(StudentNo) As Integer
```

where *StudentNo* is a value collected from the user at an earlier point in the program.

2.14 Controls as variables

It is important to note that the values stored in controls are accessible to other parts of a program, and can therefore be used as an alternative to variables. When the user types something into a Text Box, it is stored in the **Text** property. This can be used by code attached to the Text Box, or to any other control. The line:

```
Label1.Caption = Text1.Text
```

would copy whatever was in the Text Box into the Label.

Every control has one main property, and this is always the obvious one – the Caption of a Label, the Text of a Text Box, the Picture in a Picture Box or an Image, the Value of a Scroll Bar. You do not have to specify this property when you want to read or change its value, though your code may be clearer if you do. Thus:

```
Label1 = Text1
```

would have exactly the same effect as the earlier line.

The main properties of controls are listed in Appendix B.

2.15 Exercises

1. Set up a form containing a Text Box, a Label and a button. Write a Caption on the Label asking the user to enter a name. Edit the Text Box's Text property to leave it blank. Attach code to the button so that when the button is clicked, the Label displays the user's name.

2. Add a button that will end the program when clicked. The only code needed in the Click procedure is the single word **End**.

3. Edit the various Font properties of the Label, to give large, bright text on a striking background.

4. Set up a new form containing one Label and three Command Buttons. Edit the button captions to read "Stop", "Go" and "End". Attach code to these buttons so that the first makes the Label display "Stop" in red, the second makes it display "Go" in green, and the third ends the program.

Possible solutions to Exercises 1 and 4 are given in Appendix A.

3 Designing and creating programs

3.1 Program design

The traditional methods of program design, such as JSP, flowcharts, top-down design, work well for traditional programming languages. With these, the program forms a continuous whole with a distinct structure and sequence of activities. The sequence may branch or loop, but there is always something happening – even if it is only waiting for an input. With an event-driven, object-oriented language like Visual Basic, a different approach is needed.

In Visual Basic, most operations are executed in response to an event linked to an object, and at any one point there could be a number of events which could occur. The operation may be set to run its full course, or be left open to interruption by other events. The event may be, for example, a keyboard input, the movement or click of a mouse, a timer reaching its critical point or the loading of a form. When the operation is complete, the program reverts to *idle-time* – waiting for something to happen.

You don't have to write code to trap these events, for this is handled by the Visual Basic system. There are low-level routines already in place to scan the keyboard, the mouse, the timers and other sources of events. Your job is to specify what happens next, in response to those events.

While most events will be activated by the user, they can also be triggered from within the program itself. The design method must be capable of handling this interplay of objects, events and operations. Let's see how it works in practice.

3.2 The Launch program

This first program, designed to launch you into Visual Basic, shows several different examples of this interplay. I hope that it also shows how little code is needed to create good effects – in this case, a rocket launch.

The launch is produced by changing the **Top** property (which determines the vertical position) of a control to make it move up the screen. Other effects are also produced by changing properties during the execution of the program. Some of these have a fundamental impact. Notice the way that **Enabled** can be set to *False*, so that a control will no longer respond to events, and **Visible** set to *False*, to make a control disappear.

Before you start, take a few minutes to go into Paint or Paintbrush and draw yourself a rocket! Make it fairly small, then select the rocket image and save it as a bitmap (BMP) file, using **Edit | Copy To**.

3.3 The user interface

This is not just a fancy term for the screen display, though that is part of the interface. It also covers how the program interacts with the user. How does the user input data, and what information is returned to the user? In designing the form, we have to think in terms of what controls are needed and how they should be arranged for best effect. With the launch program, we want the user to be able to set the flight speed, to launch the rocket, to start again from the beginning and to exit from the program.

Launch, restart and exit are all simple jobs that can be handled neatly by Command buttons. The launch cannot take place until the speed has been set, so that button must be turned off at first. The *Enabled* property will let us do this. Setting the speed could be done in a number of ways, of which the simplest is probably to type it into a Text Box.

Some instructions are needed and can be written into a Label. This same label could also be used for the title, replacing the Caption with the instructions once the user starts the program. If the instructions are not there at first, then the speed Text Box is probably best out of the way too. The *Visible* property gives us control of this.

Last but not least, we must have something to handle the rocket. Graphics can be placed directly on the Form, but cannot be moved, so that's no good. They can also be held by Picture Boxes or Images. An Image is the best solution here. It is a much simpler control than a Picture Box, which can do a great deal more than handle graphics. It uses less memory, puts less of a strain on the system and can therefore be moved more smoothly.

Having decided what controls are needed, we can plan their layout. This is best done on paper first, as part of the overall planning process. While you are thinking out where things will go, you should also be thinking about how they will interact, and jotting down notes on the plan. (See Figure 3.1.) The design for the code should then grow naturally out of the form design.

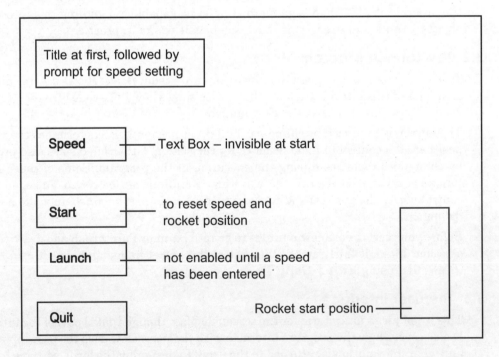

Figure 3.1 The paper plan for the Launch program, with notes on key events and changes to be made to properties.

3.4 Code design

The code here is almost entirely concerned with changing properties. The lines for this all take the shape:

control.property = newvalue

(Note the full stop between the control name and the property. *newvalue* must be enclosed in quotes if it is text.)

As long as you know the name of the control, the property that you want to change and the new value, these lines present no problems. You can explore the changes by testing them in the Properties window, while you are working on the Form design.

We can plan the code with a simple top-down design. With the three buttons, the code will be activated by the **Click** event.

Start button

reset the Rocket's **Top** to place it near the bottom of the Form
turn off the Launch button's **Enabled**
change the label **Caption** to "Enter speed then press Launch"
make the speed Text Box **Visible**, and with a **Text** of "0"
place the cursor in the Text Box, ready for the user

That last action will be achieved by the line:

txtSpeed.SetFocus

The **SetFocus** method prepares a control for keyboard input. Used on a Text Box, it places the cursor there; used on a Command Button, it highlights it and sets it so that pressing [Enter] acts the same as a mouse click. It is not essential here, for the users can put the cursor in the Text Box themselves, but it makes life easier for them.

Launch button

start to loop
subtract the **speed** value from the the Rocket's **Top** to move it up
check for other events
loop back until the Rocket is off the screen

Here we can use a **Do Loop** to keep the rocket moving. The basic structure is:

Do
    ...
Loop Until test

This will make the program cycle round the enclosed lines until the test proves true, and here the test will check the Rocket's Top value. (See Chapter 4 for more on loops.)

Unless we do something about it, the execution will lock into the loop until it reaches its end. As we want our users to be able to change the speed or restart the launch while the rocket is in flight, we must make the system check for these events, within the loop. The solution is provided by the **DoEvents** statement. This returns control to the system. If an event has occurred, it will respond to that event before going back into the loop.

Quit button

end the program

All we need here is the **End** statement that we met earlier.

Speed text box

enable the Launch button when something is typed in

Among the events handled by Text Boxes are **Keypress** and **Change**, both of which are triggered by the user typing in data. **Keypress** raises issues that are best left until later. **Change** can cope with all we want here. It will pick up any activity in the Text Box, and we can assume that the user is typing in a valid value. (If we were trying to make this program idiot-proof, we should not assume anything.)

3.5 The form and the controls

The first job is to layout the control on the form. In this case, they can go anywhere that pleases you, as long as you keep a clear flightpath for the rocket. The next job is to set their initial properties – including their Names.

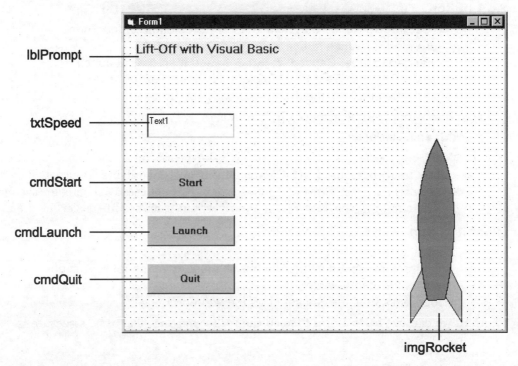

Figure 3.2 The Launch form, showing the controls and their names.

Naming controls

If a control is going to be used actively by the program, it should be given a meaningful name to replace the default Label1, Text2 or whatever. The name should be a reminder of the nature of the control and its purpose in the program. The Visual Basic manual suggests that names should start with a standard prefix to indicate the control, followed by one or more words, all run together but starting with capitals, e.g. *cmdQuit*. A list of recommended prefixes is given in Appendix B.

In this program we have Command Button (*cmd*), Text Box (*txt*), Label (*lbl*) and Image (*img*). The names are shown above in Figure 3.2.

Setting properties

Type in the Captions for the Command Buttons and the Label, setting fonts and other decorative properties as you like.

Set the *txtSpeed*.**Visible** property to *False*. It will have no obvious effect at this stage, but *txtSpeed* will be visible when the program is run, and will only appear when the property is reset to *True* by the Start button.

Set the *cmdLaunch*.**Enabled** property to *False*. When the program starts, its Caption will be displayed in grey, rather than black, and the button will not respond to a click. It will be enabled again by the Change event on *txtSpeed*.

To get the picture into *imgRocket*, select the **Picture** property of the control and click the [...] button to open this dialog box:

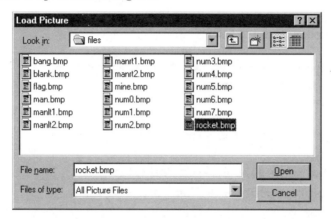

Work your way through the Folders to get to the right place, then select the graphic from the list of files. Click **Open** to load the file into the control and to exit from the dialog box.

3.6 Writing the code

To attach code to an object's event, double-click on the object to open its code window. As this opens ready to take code into the most commonly used event – such as **Click** for a Command Button, you should not need to do anything else.

Start with **cmdStart**, and type in the lines shown here – ignoring the lines starting with a quote. Those are **comment** to help explain the code. In this book, the comments are shown in lighter text than the active parts of the code. On the screen, comments are usually shown in green. Comments can be written at the end of active lines, or on lines by themselves – the system simply ignores everything after a single quote.

Do not include the first or last lines – they will be in place already.

Press [Enter] at the end of each line.

The system will then check your typing and alert you to any errors.

- Some errors will not be spotted. If you mistype the name of a control, Visual Basic will assume that you mean another control or a variable. If you have started a loop with a *Do* line, but omitted the *Loop Until* at the end, the system will not spot this either, for it is only checking individual lines at this stage.

```
Private Sub cmdStart_Click ()
    imgRocket.Top = 3000
    lblPrompt.Caption = "Enter speed then press Launch"
    ' make the Speed Text box appear
    txtSpeed.Visible = True
    txtSpeed.Text = "0"
    ' turn off the Launch button
    cmdLaunch.Enabled = False
    ' place the cursor in the Speed Text box
    txtSpeed.SetFocus
End Sub
```

When the **cmdStart_Click** code is done, click back onto the Form and double-click the next control to which you want to add code.

```
Private Sub cmdLaunch_Click ()
    Do
        imgRocket.Top = imgRocket.Top - txtSpeed.Text
        ' check for other events
        DoEvents
        ' this should be well clear of the form
    Loop Until imgRocket.Top < -5000
End Sub
```

Note the line that changes the Rocket's **Top** value.

```
imgRocket.Top = imgRocket.Top - txtSpeed.Text
```

We want to subtract from it the number held in the **Text** property of the *txtSpeed* box. This is not actually *Text*, but a *Variant* data type, which can be treated as either Text or a Number value. As we are using it here in a calculation, Visual Basic realises that we want its numeric value, and handles it accordingly.

```
Private Sub txtSpeed_Change ()
    cmdLaunch.Enabled = True            ' turn on the Launch button
End Sub
```

```
Private Sub cmdQuit_Click ()
    End
End Sub
```

3.7 Save your work

Before you attempt to run the program, save it. Visual Basic is a very robust system, and I have never had a program crash so badly that the computer has needed resetting, but there is always a first time.

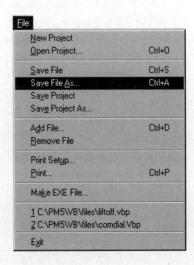

- First use **File | Save File As** to save the form. When the dialog box opens, check that you are pointing to the right disk and folder, and type in a suitable title, such as *"Launch"* – don't bother to type the *".FRM"* extension as it is added automatically.

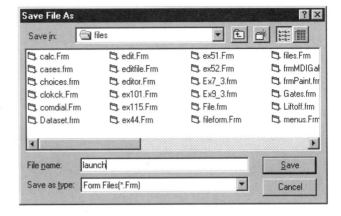

When saving a Form FIle or a Project, just type the name and let Visual Basic add the correct extension.

- Next use **File | Save Project As** to save the whole program. You can call this *"Launch"* as well. The system will add a *".Vbp"* extension, which will distinguish the project from the form file.

3.8 Running and testing

Set the program in motion with the **Run | Start** command, or by clicking the ▶ icon. The system checks your code again, and this time it looks at the interaction between the different lines. If any errors are noted, it will open the relevant code window with the error highlighted.

Play with the program. Set the speed and launch the rocket. Use the Start button to reset the rocket on its pad. Try changing the speed, or restarting, while the rocket is in motion. Test every possible sequence of events.

While you are doing this, think about what is happening beneath the surface, about the interplay between the objects as events are handled. Take any point in the program and note what events are waiting to happen. For instance, after Start has been pressed, there are three events which could be triggered:

cmdStart_Click, which would get you back to where you were;

txtSpeed_Change, which would enable the Launch button, while setting the speed;

cmdQuit_Click, which would end the program.

Task 3.1   Quit from the program and back at the design screen, double-click the Launch button to open its code window. Type a single quote at the start of the **DoEvents** line. When you move the cursor off this line, the text will change colour to show that this is now a comment – not an active part of the code.

Run the program again and try to restart, or change the speed, while the rocket is in motion. You should find that it is impossible. Without **DoEvents**, the system cannot trap events when it is executing code.

3.9 Making an EXE file

When you have finished developing the program, you may like to create a free-standing executable version of it. The program can then be run direct from Windows, rather than only through the Visual Basic system. As with most other things in Visual Basic, the hard work is all done for you.

1. Open the **File** menu and select **Make EXE file**.

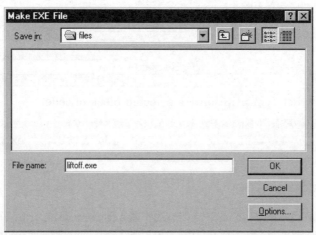

Figure 3.3 The Make EXE file dialog box as we start to make the first one.

2. The **File name** will be the same as the name of the project, but with an .EXE extension. Before you click **OK** to save it, click the **Options** button.

3. When the **Options** dialog box opens, you should find that most of the details have been filled in correctly by the system. You may want to change the **Application Title**, the label that will appear beneath the icon on in Program Manager or Windows Explorer.

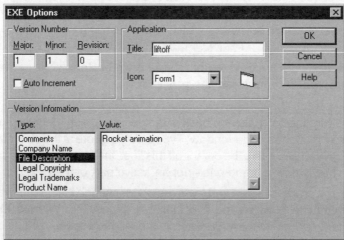

Figure 3.4 The Options dialog box when making an EXE file.

4. You will not be able to change the **icon** at this point. It is only possible if you have assigned an alternative image to the Icon property of the Form. Icons can be selected for this from the VB\ICONS directory, if they have been installed.

3.10 Printouts

In Visual Basic, there are three aspects of a program that can be printed – the *Code*, the *Form* and the *Form Text*.

The **Code** is what you would expect – the lines of Basic program – and note that all working procedures are printed out, one after the other.

The **Form Image** printout is a copy of the on-screen display – or the nearest equivalent that your printer can manage,

The **Form As Text** details the settings of the Properties of the form and of any objects on it. This is the least useful of the three as most of the settings are visible on the Form printout.

The **Range** to be printed can be:

Selection – which will print only a selected block of code.

Current Module is the form or Basic module that was selected when you called up the Print command.

All will print all the forms and modules in the program.

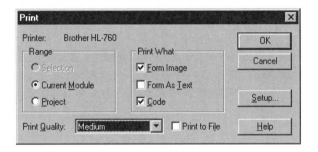

To get your printouts, select the form, or the block of code that you want to print, and take the menu sequence **File | Print**. At the dialog box, select the **Range** then tick the **Print What** check boxes as required.

3.11 Exercises

1. Using the techniques illustrated in the Launch program, design and build a program that will move across the screen. For a more impressive display, create a background picture and drop this into the Picture property of the Form.

2. The aim here is to produce an annotated diagram. Set up a Form with a large Image above and a large Label below. Draw or scan a picture of a computer, save the file and load it into the Image's Picture. Place small Command buttons beside key components on the Image, with the Captions set to match the components. Attach code to each of these buttons, so that when clicked, they display information about the component in the Label.

3. Write a program to convert temperatures from Celsius to Fahrenheit, using the formula:

    DegreesF = DegreesC * 9 / 5 + 32

Hint:	Use Text Boxes to take the input in Celsius and display the result in Fahrenheit. The conversion code can be attached to the Change event of the Celsius Text Box, or to the Click event of a button (captioned "Convert"). Include a Quit Button on the Form, to end the program.

4. Adapt the last program so that it can convert temperatures from either form to the other. To change Fahrenheit to Celsius use the formula:

DegreesC = (DegreesF – 32) * 5 / 9

Hint:	If you try to run the conversion routines from the Change events of both Text Boxes, you will hit a snag. As each Change routine would alter the value in the other Text Box, it would trigger its Change event and alter the value in the box that was being typed in – chaos! Use suitably captioned command buttons instead.

Possible solutions to Exercises 3 and 4 are given in Appendix A.

4 Program flow

Controlling the flow

The overall flow of a program is largely controlled by the user's interaction with the screen objects, as we noted in the last chapter and to which we shall return again, but if anything interesting is to happen when an object is selected, we must control the flow of execution within routines. This can be considered under two main headings – *branches* and *loops*.

With a branch, the execution will flow down one of two or more paths, depending upon the result of a logical test. The relevant structures here are **If ... Then ... Else** (and variants), and **Select Case**. The **GoTo** and **GoSub** jumps may be used in conjunction with **If** to skip over a set of lines. GoTo is reviled by purists as its use can lead to horribly tangled code, but there are times when it offers a convenient solution. GoSub takes the flow off to a subroutine.

With loops – the iteration of a block of code – the number of repetitions may be controlled by a logical test, using one of the many variations of the **Do ... Loop**. Where the loop is to run a fixed number of times, the **For ... Next** structure offers the simplest solution.

4.1 Logical testing

Logical tests may be performed upon string or numeric *expressions*, or upon controls. (The latter raises complications that we will not dwell on here.) The expressions – string or numeric – may contain variables, literal values, functions and arithmetic or other operators, as long as the expressions produce suitable values. Examples of typical expressions:

Surname, X, Y	Variables, used alone
"LETMEIN", 99, 0	Literal Values
X * 2	Calculations including Variables and Values
LEN(Zword), CHR(Num)	Functions producing numeric or string values

A test will result in either a *True, False* or *Null* value. Null occurs when one or more of the expressions being tested has a null value, i.e. it involves a variable that does not hold any value. For most purposes, Null and False can be taken as the same.

Logical tests usually involve the comparison operators, e.g. *If X > 1000* ... but can be performed directly on an expression. The test *If X Then...* would be True if X held any non-zero value.

Comparison operators

Visual Basic supports the usual set of relational, or comparison operators, plus two unique to the language:

=	Equal to	<>	Greater or Less than (not Equal to)
<	Less than	>	Greater than
<=	Less than or Equal to	>=	Greater than or Equal to
Like	'Fuzzy' string comparisons	**Is**	Compares control variables

Functions and arithmetic operators have a higher priority than comparison operators, which means that expressions are evaluated before the test.

Test	Value	Why?
99 <= 10 * 5	False	10 * 5 = 50 which is less than 99
LEN("Fred") < 10	True	"Fred" has 4 characters

When used with string expressions, the operators compare the characters by their ASCII values, and only travel as far down the string as is necessary to make the comparison. This can lead to apparently unusual results.

Test	Value	Why?
"A" < "B"	True	ASCII "A" = 65 and ASCII "B" = 66
"a" < "B"	False	ASCII "a" = 97
"Bee" < "Beekeeper"	True	They are equal up to "Bee", but the second goes on, and any character is greater than nothing.
"Anteater" > "ant"	False	ASCII "A" = 65, ASCII "a" = 97
"99" < "100"	False	String comparison, ASCII "9" = 57, ASCII "1" = 48
Val("99")<Val("100")	True	Functions yield number values

Where numbers are taken from Text Boxes, or from variables that have not been given a type, they are variants and may well behave as strings. When in doubt, use **Val()** to force the conversion from string to number.

Like

This allows you to make inexact matches, finding strings that only have some characters in common. The comparisons are made using *wildcards* – special characters that can stand for any other single character or set. The wildcards are:

?	Any single character
#	Any single digit
*	Zero or more characters
[*set*]	Any character in the set defined by its first and last character
[!*set*]	Any character except those in the defined list

Some examples may help.

Surname Like "Sm?th"	True for "Smith" and "Smyth"
Fname Like "*.DTA"	True for any file with ".DTA" extension
Digit Like "[0-9]"	True for any digit, but no other characters
LowLetter Like "[a-z]"	True for any single lower-case letter
PicNum Like "Fig[0-9]"	True for "Fig0", "Fig1", "Fig2", etc
NonDigit Like "[!0-9]"	True for anything except the digits

Note that there are quotes around the whole expression.

Is can only be used with control variables and raises points that are too complex to deal with at this level.

Logical operators

There are six logical operators, which are mainly used to combine two or more relational operations in a test. If you have programmed in Pascal or a traditional Basic, you may have met some of these before, but some will be quite new.

NOT   Used with a single expression, to reverse its value, so that True becomes False and vice versa.

AND   Links two expressions and is True if both expressions are True.

OR   True if either or both expressions are True.

XOR   (Exclusive OR) True if one or other – but not both – expressions are True.

EQU   (Equivalence) True if both expressions are True or both are False.

IMP   (Implication) True if both are the same, as EQU, or if only the second is True; False only when the first expression is True and the second is False. I have yet to find a use for this one.

Where a test uses two or more logical operators, they are evaluated is the same order in which they are listed above.

Examples of logical operations:

... X > 1000 AND Y > 1000...

True if both X and Y are over their limits

...X > 1000 XOR Y > 1000...

Brackets in logical tests

If you want to change the priority – perhaps to evaluate an OR before an AND – enclose the OR part in brackets.

True if either of them are over their limits, but False if they both are over (or below).

...NOT (X > 1000 EQU Y > 1000)

This gives exactly the same results as the previous test – work it out and see.

...X > 100 AND Y > 100 OR X < 0...

True if either X and Y are both over their limits, or X is negative – in which case the Y is irrelevant.

...Y > 100 AND (X > 100 OR X < 0)...

True if Y is over 100 and X is above or below its limits.

4.2 Branching with If

Though based on the **If.. Then.. Else...** test found in most other languages, Visual Basic's version has several variations and traps for the unwary. In all cases, **If** is followed by some form of logical test and the keyword **Then**. What happens next varies.

Single line branching

Where only a small amount of code is dependent upon the test, the whole structure can be conveniently written on a single line, following one or other of these patterns.

   If *test* Then *statement(s)-if-true*

   If *test* Then *statement(s)-if-true* Else *statement(s)-if-false*

Examples:

If age < 16 Then status = "Junior"

If password = "letmein" Then Msgbox "Hello" Else Msgbox "Goodbye" : End

In the first example, nothing happens if the *age* value is 16 or more. In the second, the presence of the **Else** clause means that action is taken if a wrong password is given. The action here consists of two statements, one producing a message, the other ending the program. Note that where there are several statements, they are separated by colons (:).

Multi-line Ifs

There is no theoretical limit to the number of statements you can include in a single-line *If* structure, for the whole line can be as long as you like. In practice, long lines are awkward to view on screen and likely to be a source of error, simply because you cannot see clearly what they are doing.

If more than one statement is dependent upon the truth or falsity of the test, it is best to split the structure over several lines.

...If *test* Then
   statement-if-true-1
   statement-if-true-2
   ...
Else *statement-if-false-1*
   statement-if-false-2
   ...
End If

Note the **End If** at the end of the structure. This is not needed with a single line *If*, but essential with the multi-line variant. If you prefer, the first statement after *Else* can be pushed down to the next line. This can make a routine more readable.

A simple multi-line **If** might look like this:

If age < 16 Then
   Status = "Junior"
   ClubFees = 7.5
Else
   Status = "Senior"
   ClubFees = 25
End If

In this case, both **Status** and **ClubFees** are dependent upon the age of the member, with only two alternatives, based on the 16 limit.

ElseIf

Where there are several alternative routes to the flow, the structure can be extended by an **ElseIf** clause – or by more than one **ElseIf** – each followed by its own logical test and a **Then**.

Try this example. Write it into the **Click** procedure of a blank Form, run the program, click on the form and type in a value.

```
Private Sub Form_Click ()
    Dim salary As Single
    salary = InputBox("How much do you want to earn?")
    If salary > 50000 Then
        MsgBox "Don't go into writing"
    ElseIf salary > 20000 Then
        MsgBox "Good luck"
    Else
        MsgBox "What modest aims!"
    End If
End Sub
```

This form of the structure is appropriate where you want to test a value against several limits, or where you have second and subsequent tests that are only to be performed if the first one proves false.

Nested Ifs

The statement that follows **Then** or **Else** can be another **If** structure. This can be a single-line or a multi-line one – in which case it must be closed by its own **End If**. These can get complicated. It is all too easy to lose track of which **End If** relates to which **If**. Good layout will help to keep things clearer. You may have noticed that I have indented the statements in the examples above, so that structure stands out. Where one If structure is nested within another, its keywords should be indented, keeping the **If**, **Else** and **End If** in line, and their statements indented further.

If layout is important for displaying the structure after you have written it, design is crucial for getting right in the first place. Start by drawing up a JSP diagram, or decision tree in some form, so that you are clear about the logic and the nature of each branch.

For example, suppose you wanted a routine that would work out the correct form of address, based on the user's age and sex. (We will ignore marital status and address all adult females as 'Ms'.)

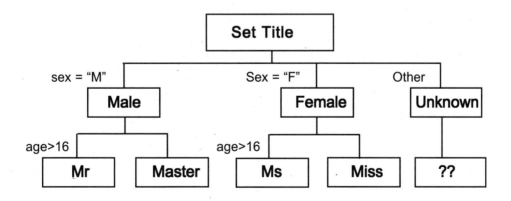

Figure 4.1 JSP diagram for a form-of-address routine.

Task 4.1 Write a routine to implement this design, using nested Ifs. Type it into a Form_Click procedure and test out each branch. A possible solution is given at the end of the chapter.

4.3 Select Case

Where you have many alternative routes all based on the values that may be held in one variable, the **Select Case** structure provides a clearer solution than a set of **If**'s or one long multi-branched **If**. The basic shape is:

```
Select Case variable
    Case values_1
        actions if variable = values_1
        further actions if variable = values_1
    Case value_2
        actions if variable = values_2
    ...
    ...
    Case Else
        actions if variable = any other value
End Select
```

The layout is important. Each *Case* must be on a new line, and the actions that follow from a *Case* must start on a line below – they cannot be run along the same line.

```
        Case Value_1  actions ...
```

This will produce an error report.

Any string or numeric variable can be used in a **Select Case**. The values that follow each **Case** can be a single item, a range joined by the keyword **To**, or a set of alternatives linked by commas.

Case Else is optional, but a good way to handle unexpected values. Note that the structure must be closed by **End Select**.

This block of code is taken from the Maths Test program, given in full in Chapter 5. It shows the structure at its simplest. The values in the variable *sumtype* can only be "+", "-", "*" or "/" and each initiates a single action.

```
Select Case sumtype
    Case "+"
        z = x + y
    Case "-"
        z = x – y
    Case "*"
        z = x * y
    Case "/"
        z = x / y
End Select
```

Worked example

A more complex **Select Case** structure is shown below. This handles single values, ranges and sets. It takes in a character through an InputBox, and delivers a different message depending upon the nature of the character.

```
Private Sub Form_Click ()
    Dim char As String

    char = InputBox("Enter a character")

    Select Case char
        Case "!"                      'single value
            MsgBox "Shriek", 48
            End                       ' exit from the program
        Case "0" To "9"               'range "0" to  "9" inclusive
        MsgBox "Digit"
        Case "A" To "Z", "a" To "z"   'two ranges, capitals and lower case
            MsgBox "Letter"
        Case "(", "(", "{", "}", "[", "]"   'set of alternatives
            MsgBox "Bracket"
        Case Else                     'for everything else
            MsgBox "Symbol ASCII Code " & Asc(char)
    End Select
End Sub
```

Input actually is !

Task 4.2	Copy the code into a Form's Click procedure. Test it with a range of values that will activate each *Case*. What happens if you enter a word instead of a single character?

4.4 GoTo

This is only included for the sake of completeness and because there are some dyed-in-the-wool Basic programmers who could not contemplate life without it. The simple fact is that **GoTo** tends to produce poor, tangled code and is not necessary except in **Resume** statements (See Chapter 6). Anything that you can do with a **GoTo**, you can do better and more easily in another way. If you want to repeat a set of lines, use a **For ... Next** or a **Loop** (see below Section 4.5). If you want to bypass a block of code, it is neater and simpler to make the block into a procedure, (see Chapter 8).

But if you really must use **GoTo**, here's how. The jump can be forwards or backwards, but must be in the same procedure. Mark the target point in the code with a label. This can be a number or a word, written with a following colon. It can be on a separate line above, or at the start of the line containing the first statement in the target block.

The **GoTo** can be written as a single-line statement or incorporated into an **If ... Then** It is followed by the label name – without the colon.

For example, here are two **GoTo**s – one used to repeat a set of lines, the other to jump out of the loop when the target value is reached. Compare this tangled code with the more elegant **Loop**s shown below.

```
Private Sub Form_Load ()
    Dim x As Integer
    Form1.Show          'ensure the form is visible
    x = 0
startloop:
    x = x + 1
    Form1.Print x
    If x = 10 Then GoTo endloop
    GoTo startloop
endloop:
    MsgBox "Done"
    End
End Sub
```

4.5 For ... Next

Visual Basic's *For ... Next* structure is almost the same as that of traditional Basics, and more flexible than Pascal's. In this formal definition, optional features are enclosed in [brackets]. You will note that much is optional:

```
For variable = start_value To end_value [Step size]
    statements...
    [Exit For]
    statements...
Next [variable]
```

Start_value and *end_value* can be any numbers, variables or expressions that produce suitable values. They do not have to be integer. If the **Step** *size* is omitted, the loop counter will be increased by one each time, otherwise the Step can be any whole or fractional value, either positive or negative. The variable name after the **Next** is not essential, but does make the code easier to read.

Exit For provides an escape route, should you need to break out of the loop before the end value has been reached. As you would normally use **For ... Next** loops to run through a fixed range of values, this feature will rarely be wanted.

Nested loops

For ... Next loops can be nested within one another. Indenting your code, and writing the variable names in the **Next** lines will help to ensure that inner loops are indeed completed within the outer ones.

A **For ... Next** loop can be as simple as this:

```
For num = 1 To 10
    Form1.Print num
Next
```

Or it may use all the 'optional extras', as in this next example.

```
Private Sub Form_Click ()
    Dim num, stars, x
    Form1.Cls
    For num = 1 To 8 Step .5          ' partial Step
        x = Rnd(1) * 100
```

```
        For stars = 1 To x                  ' variable for end value
            Form1.Print "*";
            If stars > 50 Then Exit For     ' forced exit
        Next stars
        Form1.Print x
    Next num
End Sub
```

Task 4.3   Copy the code into a Form's Click procedure. Run the program and click on the form to see the display. It should match the one shown below. How could you simplify the For... lines and still get the same results?

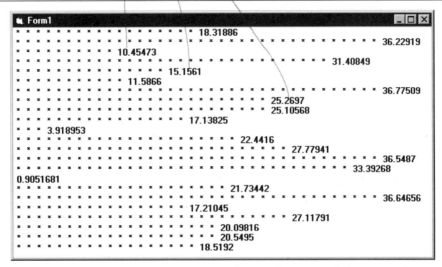

Figure 4.2 The screen display from the nested loops code.

4.6 Do Loops

These offer the most flexible way to repeat a set of lines. We used the **Do ... Loop Until** version in the last chapter, but the structure has a number of variations. They can be summarised in these formats:

1. **Do Until** or **While** *test*

     statements ...

     ... [Exit Do]

     Loop

2. **Do**

     statements ...

     ... [Exit Do]

     Loop Until or **While** *test*

Some things remain the same – there is always a **Do** at the start and **Loop** at the end, and there must be an exit test somewhere, or the loop will run until it crashes the system.

If the exit test is written in the **Do** line, the loop will not be executed if the test is satisfied; written into the **Loop** line, the loop will be executed at least once.

In either position, the test may use either the **Until** or **While** keyword. The two are effectively the same, except that the logic of a **While** test is reversed. **While** *test* is the same as **Until Not** *test*. Use whichever gives the clearest logic test.

As a final option, you can omit the test from either start or end and rely on an *Exit Do* to break out of the loop. This would normally be activated with an *If* test.

The following loops all produce exactly the same results. Notice how the comparison operators and test values vary to suit the **Until** or **While** expressions.

Test at the start

```
num = 1
Do Until num = 11
    Print num
    num = num + 1
Loop
```

or

```
num = 1
Do While num <= 10
    Print num
    num = num + 1
Loop
```

Test at the end

```
num = 1
Do
    Print num
    num = num + 1
Loop Until num = 11
```

or

```
num = 1
Do
    Print num
    num = num + 1
Loop While num <= 10
```

Test in the middle

```
num = 1
Do
    Print num
    If num = 10 Then Exit Do
    num = num + 1
Loop
```

4.7 While ... Wend

I suspect that this structure is present mainly for compatibility with earlier Basics, as it provides nothing that cannot be done as well – or better – with a **Do While** Loop.

The syntax is simple:

> **While** *test*
> > *statements*
>
> **Wend**

While ...Wend structures can be nested, as can any Loops, but there is no means of forcing an early exit.

4.8 Exercises

1. Take the **ElseIf** example routine from section 3 and rewrite it as a set of single line **If** structures. Note that the branch handled there by the **ElseIf** clause will need a compound **AND** test.

2. Write a program using two nested **For ... Next** loops that will produce one or other of these patterns:

```
* 1                        8 ********
** 2                       7 *******
*** 3                      6 ******
**** 4                     5 *****
***** 5                    4 ****
****** 6                   3 ***
******* 7                  2 **
******** 8                 1 *
```

3. Design and write a times tables tester. It should ask users what table they want to be tested on, then set a series of random problems from that table. If the user gets an answer wrong, the program should display the table before asking the next question.

Hint: Random numbers can be produced by the Rnd function. This generates decimal fractions in the range 0 to 1. Multiply this by 10 to move the range on to 0 to 9.999, and use the Int function to convert the result to an integer. The random number line should read something like:

> **x = Int(Rnd * 10) + 1**

The times table can be written directly on the Form using the Print method, but do a Cls first to clear it, or you will find that the print position moves steadily down and off the form.

---

4. A health and fitness club has four levels of membership charges, based on the age of the member. 0-16 (Juniors) and 55-80 (Seniors) are both charged at half the 17-54 (Adult) rate of £250 p.a. Members aged 81 or over (Honorary) are allowed in free. Using a **Select Case** structure, write a program that will ask for the member's age, and display the membership category and charges.

Solutions to all these exercises are given in Appendix A.

4.9 Solution to Task 4.1

```
Private Sub Form_Click
    Dim sex, title As String
    Dim age As Integer
    sex = InputBox("Enter sex (M/F)")
    age = InputBox("Enter age ")
    If sex = "M" Then
        If age > 16 Then title = "Mr" Else title = "Master"      ' first nested If
    ElseIf sex = "F" Then
        If age > 16 Then                                          ' start of second
            title = "Ms"
        Else title = "Miss"
        End If                                                    ' end of second
    Else
        MsgBox "Sex Unknown"
        title = "??"
    End If                                                        ' end of outer If
    MsgBox "Your form of address is " & title
End Sub
```

5 Interacting with the user

One of the main planks of the Windows philosophy is that applications should be user-friendly. With this in mind, its designers have provided menus, icons, buttons, scroll bars and other tools which can simplify the interaction with the user. These tools are available to us in Visual Basic, and we should make full use of them in our programming. Sometimes keyboard entry – the only form of input available in many traditional programming languages – is the most appropriate way to get data from the user. At other times you can make life easier for the user, and reduce the need for error-checking in your program, by asking the user to select from a list, check an option, slide a scroll bar or click on a button. Explore the alternatives, and whenever you want input, consider which method will be simplest for the user. A Windows application should be intuitive to use, so take as your rule "if it feels right, it must be right."

5.1 MsgBoxes

We have already made use of the InputBox and MsgBox facilities briefly, but both have additional features that should not be overlooked. A MsgBox can be used for input as well as output, and its message can be reinforced by a bright symbol; default values can be set for InputBoxes and both can carry titles.

Outputs via the MsgBox statement

When used for output, **MsgBox** takes this form:

> MsgBox *message, typecode, title*

Both the *message* and *title* are strings, and can be straight text (in quotes), variables, string functions or combinations of these, joined by ampersands (&). If you want the message to spread over more than one line, include the newline and carriage return characters (ASCII 10 and 13) in the text. The simplest way to do this is to define a newline variable and incorporate that in the message. (See example below.)

The *typecode* is a number formed by adding together the codes that control which buttons are to appear, which symbol is to be displayed and which button is to be highlighted when the box opens.

For example, to get a warning symbol, OK and Cancel buttons, with Cancel (the second button) set as the default, you would need the typecode 1 + 48 + 256. This could be written into the statement as the expression **1 + 48 + 256**, or as the total **305**.

Typecodes

Button codes

0	OK
1	OK and Cancel
2	Abort, Retry and Ignore
3	Yes, No and Cancel
4	Yes and No
5	Retry and Cancel

Symbols

0	None
16	![X symbol]
32	![? symbol]
48	![! symbol]
64	![i symbol]

Default button

0	First
256	Second
512	Third

Where MsgBox is only being used for output, the buttons are irrelevant, so the only valid typecodes are 0, 16, 32, 48 and 64.

The box shown here was produced by the code given below. Note the use of the *NL* variable, that holds the line feed and carriage return characters, to produce a two-line message, and the 64 typecode which gives the Information symbol. To test this, and later examples, type the code into the **Form_Click** procedure, then run the program and click on the Form to watch them work.

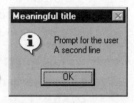

```
Dim NL, message, title As String
Dim typecode As Integer

NL = Chr(10) & Chr(13)                        'New Line characters

message = "Prompt for the user " & NL & "A second line"
typecode = 64                          ' info graphic
title = "Meaningful Title"
MsgBox message, typecode, title
```

(handwritten annotations: This isn't necessary if Chr(10) & Chr(13) are put in directly • here instead • This is necessary*)*

Note: If no symbol is wanted, the typecode can be omitted altogether – though if you do want to include a title, you must put in an extra comma, for the system expects the title to be the *third* item in the list, e.g.

```
MsgBox message,, title
```

Inputs via the MsgBox function

If you want to collect a reply from a MsgBox, it must be used in its *function* form.

result = MsgBox(*prompt, typecode, title*)

This differs from the statement in two ways. The first is obvious – it returns a value to the program, and this must be used or collected in a variable. The second is more subtle, but just as important – the parameters after **MsgBox** must be enclosed in brackets.

The value returned by the function shows which button was clicked.

Value	Button	Value	Button
1	OK	2	Cancel
3	Abort	4	Retry
5	Ignore	6	Yes
7	No		

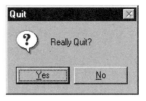

This box was defined with a typecode of 36, made up of 32 for the question mark and 4 to get the **Yes** and **No** buttons. You will see that it has been written in the code as 32 + 4. It could equally well have been written as a simple 36.

Here's the code:

```
Dim typecode As Integer
Dim reply As Integer

typecode = 32 + 4                               ' ? and Yes, No
reply = MsgBox("Really Quit? ", typecode, "Quit")   ' note the brackets
If reply = 6 Then End                           ' 6 = "Yes"
```

Task 5.1   Add a confirmation MsgBox to any existing program with a Quit button. It should carry the exclamation mark and the two-line message:

Quit selected.

Please Confirm

It should also have the OK and Cancel buttons. The code should only end the program if OK is selected.

5.2 InputBoxes

An InputBox can only ever be used in this (function) form:

result = InputBox(*prompt, title, default_value*)

Unlike **MsgBox**, **InputBox** does not take a typecode. It will always display **OK** and **Cancel**, and cannot hold symbols. The *default_value* is a string that can be displayed in the entry slot of the box, and will be returned if the user presses OK. In the example below, "-99", which is being used to mark the end of the routine, has been set as the default.

Clicking **Cancel**, or pressing the **[Esc]** key, produces a Null value, which can cause problems. The return value is of the Variant type, and so, in theory, could be collected by a number variable. If a **Cancel** has returned Null, trying to copy this into a number variable would cause an error. If you want to use **InputBox** to get a number, the safe solution is to take the input value into a string or variant, and check that something is there before passing it to the number variable.

To run the next example, you must declare a **Single** variable called *Total* in the general declaration of a form and type this code into the **Form_Click** procedure.

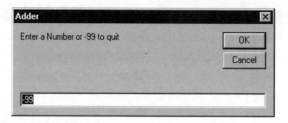

Figure 5.1 An InputBox displaying a default value.

```
Private Sub Form_Click
    Dim prompt, title As String
    Dim reply
    Dim numval As Single

    prompt = "Enter a Number or -99 to quit"
    title = "Adder"
    reply = InputBox(prompt, title, "-99")
    if reply then numval = Val(reply)
    If numval = -99 Then
        End
    Else Total = Total + numval
    End If
    MsgBox "Total so far " & Total
End Sub
```

answer

5.3 ScrollBars

ScrollBars are familiar to any Windows user and offer a convenient way of controlling a value that can vary between fixed limits. They are the obvious way, for example, of setting the Red, Blue and Green values when defining colours, (see Chapter 7), but are also an interesting alternative to keyboard input in many situations.

ScrollBars have five key properties:

Value	the position of the slider in relation to the ends
Min	the value when the slider is at the top, or left, of the bar
Max	the value when the slider is at the bottom, or right, of the bar
SmallChange	the result of clicking on an arrow
LargeChange	the result of clicking on the bar beside the slider

All values must be within the normal integer range, i.e. –32,768 to +32,767, though in practice your Min and Max are likely to be much tighter than that.

The next example uses ScrollBars to move a block around the screen – and the whole program contains only five lines of code! To try it, place these objects on a new form.

Vertical ScrollBar, down the left side

Horizontal ScrollBar, along the bottom

Frame, of a size that will fit within the limits of the scroll bars

Shape, named *shpBlock*, placed within the Frame

Command Button, captioned "Quit"

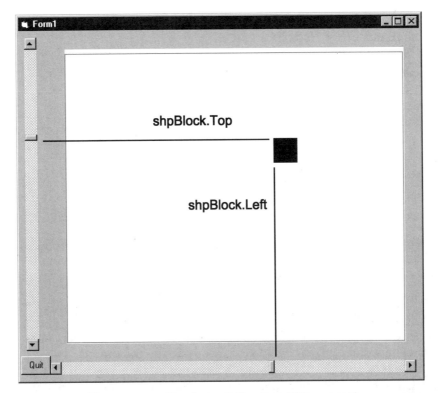

Figure 5.2 The screen display of the ScrollBar testing program.

The purpose of the frame is to provide a running area for the Block. Any object placed within a Frame cannot be moved out of it, and its Top and Left co-ordinates will be relative to the Frame, not to the Form beneath.

As the Frame's size is the same as the ScrollBars' Max values, we have a simple translation of ScrollBar values to Block co-ordinates. The Frame should be aligned as closely as possible with the ends of the ScrollBars, inside the Arrow buttons. The Max value of the VScroll control should be the same as the Height of the Frame, and the Max of the HScroll the same as the Frame's Width.

The Block merely needs to be visible on screen, and that can be achieved by changing the BackColor from white, and setting the BackStyle to Opaque. Do make sure that you place it within the Frame when you first define it.

For the code, go to the procedures listed here and type the single lines in each.

```
Private Sub VScroll1_Change ()        'handles clicks on the arrows and the bar
    shpBlock.Top = Vscroll1
End Sub
Private Sub VScroll1_Scroll ()                    'handles the dragged slider
    shpBlock.Top = Vscroll1
End Sub
Private Sub HScroll1_Change ()
    shpBlock.Left = Hscroll1
End Sub
```

```
    Private Sub HScroll1_Scroll ()
        shpBlock.Left = Hscroll1
    End Sub
    Private cmdQuit_Click
        End
    End Sub
```

Note that you do not need to specify the *Value* property when collecting the values from the scroll bars. The system assumes that this – its main property – is what you want.

5.4 Frames

A Frame by itself does very little. The chief purpose of this control is to enclose other objects, providing a sort of form within a form, as we saw in that last example. Probably their most common use is to hold sets of OptionButtons or CheckBoxes, as you will see below. Another sensible use for them is to enclose Labels and Text Boxes where the Label serves as a prompt for input into the Text Box.

When a Frame is made visible or invisible, all the objects within it appear or disappear; when it is moved, they all move with it. The latter is very useful at design time, and possibly during the execution of a program.

Once a control has been placed in a Frame, it cannot be moved out of it, either at design or runtime; nor can controls that were placed outside the Frame be moved into it. At design time it is possible to get round this limitation by using **Edit | Cut** to remove a control, and **Edit | Paste** to place it within (or outside), but you will save yourself a lot of trouble if you plan your Frames properly from the start.

5.5 OptionButtons

The OptionButtons controls are almost always used in sets, and only one can be selected at any one time. This means that you cannot have more than one set of options on one form – you may have placed them as separate sets, but the system will treat them as one. The solution is to place your OptionButtons within **Frames**, as each framed set is treated separately. These provide a nice visual touch to the display as well as being essential to the grouping of OptionButtons.

There are essentially two ways of finding out which OptionButton has been selected.

The first is to use the OptionButton's *Value* property. If an OptionButton has been selected, it will be True. You can therefore use expressions such as:

```
    If Option2 Then...
```

and the statements that follow this test will only be executed if *Option2* has been selected. This is probably the best approach where there are only two possible choices, as it leads to a neat **If ... Then ... Else ...** structure.

The alternative is to set a variable when the OptionButton is clicked. This is more suitable where there are a number of possible options, and is the approach that has been used in the following example. It deals, appropriately enough, with options, though the options in this case are subject choices.

A student must choose one language, from Option Block 1, and one creative subject, from Option Block 2. Each block is represented by a Frame on the form, and the OptionButtons have been suitably named. The variables *Choice1* and *Choice2*,

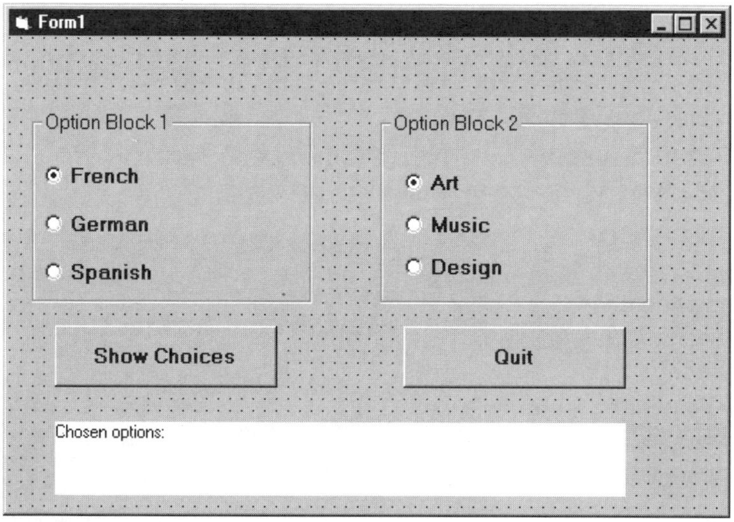

Figure 5.3 The Form design for the Options testing program.

declared in the general declarations area, are used to collect the choices. This is done by assigning values to the variables when the OptionButtons are clicked. Each OptionButton's **Click** procedure follows this pattern:

```
Private Sub optFrench_Click
    Choice1 = "French"
End Sub
```

The defaults are French and Art. These are set at design time, by selecting True for their Value property. If the Value was to be used directly in the program, no further action would be needed. As we are handling the selection through variables, we must also set default values for them. This can be done in the **Form_Load** procedure.

```
Private Sub Form_Load
    Choice1 = "French"
    Choice2 = "Art"
End Sub
```

Task 5.2   Set up a form to the design shown above. Name all the OptionButtons to match their captions, starting each name with the opt abbreviation to show that this is an OptionButton control . Attach to the OptionButtons and the Form the code discussed above, plus a procedure on the Show Button which will display the student's choices.

5.6 CheckBoxes

The key difference between **OptionButtons** and **CheckBoxes**, apart from the shape of their symbols, is that any number of CheckBoxes in a set may be True at once. You have seen them at work in Visual Basic's Print routine, where they let you control which items – Form Image, Form As Text and/or Code – to output.

As with Options, you can test the Value of a CheckBox directly. In the statement:

```
If CheckBox1 Then ...
```

the actions following *Then* would be executed if the CheckBox was True. And you *must* test the Value, even in a CheckBox's Click procedure, for the click will turn the box On *and* Off, toggling between the two states. This is different from an OptionButton, where a click always turns it on.

In the Xmas list example shown here, the user is offered a choice of presents and asked to check those that he or she would like.

It helps to make the code clearer if you name controls after their captions.
These CheckBoxes might be named chkHiFi, chkDosh, chkFerrari, chkRolex, and chkTeddy.

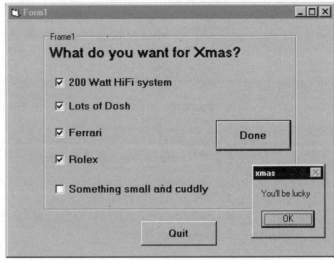

Figure 5.4 Use CheckBoxes where users can select more than one option.

The variable *gifts* is used as a counter, and increased by 1 each time a CheckBox is turned on. When the **Done** button is pressed, the code will display a different message, depending upon the greed of the user.

The Value of a CheckBox is changed as soon as it is clicked, and before the system gets to the **Click** procedure. Knowing this, we can write code for those procedures that will add to the *gifts* count if the box is checked and subtract if the click has turned it off.

```
Private Sub chkDosh_Click ()
    If chkDosh Then gifts = gifts + 1 Else gifts = gifts – 1
End Sub
```

In this simple example, the code on the **Done** button concentrates on the *gifts* total and largely ignores the states of the individual CheckBoxes. (Note the special message that is given to those who only want a teddy!) In practice, any program which used CheckBoxes would also want to react to their specific values.

```
Private Sub cmdDone_Click ()
    Dim message As String
    If gifts > 3 Then
        message = "You'll be lucky!"
    ElseIf gifts = 1 And chkTeddy Then message = "How sweet!"
    Else message = "Write to Santa"
    End If
    MsgBox message
End Sub
```

Task 5.3 Complete the example program, working from the code given above. The *gifts* variable should be declared in the general declarations area.

5.7 Menus

Look at any Windows application and you will see that it has a menu system. Why? Because it is the simplest and clearest way of showing your users the full range of facilities in your program, and of giving access to those facilities. Creating a menu is basically straightforward, though there are a few parts of the process that are not immediately obvious.

For every menu item you *must* specify:

a **caption**   If you want to enable selection by an [Alt]-keystroke combination, then type an ampersand (&) in front of the key letter. This will be underlined when displayed. The key letter is normally the first, but can be any one, and – for obvious reasons – you cannot have the same key letter for two menu items, e.g.

Caption	Display	Keystroke
&Files	**F**iles	[Alt]-[F]
E&xit	E**x**it	[Alt]-[X]

a **name**   This identifies it as a control, so that you can attach procedures to it, or set its Enabled and Visible properties from within the program.

a **position**   i.e. where it fits within your menu system – on the top bar, on a first level or lower level menu. When you create a new menu item, its caption appears in the list at the bottom of the Menu Design window. Its position within this list determines its position in the system. If set against the left edge, it will be in the top bar; if indented, it will be on the sub-menu of the non-indented item above it.

You may also set whether an item is to be **Enabled** or **Visible** when the menu first appears. These properties can be changed during execution.

To see how it fits together, we will create a menu suitable for a program that demonstrates the facilities we have covered in this chapter.

First, plan the structure on paper.

Top Bar	Choices	Dialog Boxes	Exit
	Options	InputBoxes	Yes
	Check boxes	MsgBoxes	No
	Menus	For Outputs	
		For Inputs	

Choices and **Exit** each have a first level menu; **Dialog Boxes** has a second level sub-menu opening off **MsgBoxes**.

Menu design

To create the menu select **Tools | Menu Editor**, or click on the 🖹 icon. This opens the Menu Editor. The cursor will be waiting in the **Caption** slot. Type in the Caption for the first menu item – *Choices* – with an ampersand(&) before the selection letter.

Figure 5.5 The Menu Editor.

The highlight bar in the bottom pane shows the current menu item – the one being created or edited in the top slots.

Use the mouse to select items.

Next moves the highlight bar down, creating a new item at the bottom of the list.

Insert creates a new item above the current one.

Delete removes the highlighted item from the list.

Use the mouse or the [Tab] key to move to the **Name** slot and type in a suitable control name. One that starts in "*mnu*" will help to identify it later.

Press [Enter] or click on the **Next** button. You should see that the first item has been entered into the list at the bottom and that the cursor is waiting for the next Caption.

Type in the Caption and a Name for the first option of the Choices menu – *Options*. When it appears in the list, click on the right arrow ⇥ to indent it. Indenting makes it an option on a menu rather than a header on the menu bar. Add *CheckBoxes* and *Menus* in the same way. They should indent automatically. When you get to the next header item – *Dialog Boxes* – use the left arrow ⇤ to push it back against the edge.

Add the other items for its pull-down menu, indenting once for *InputBoxes* and *MsgBoxes*, then forcing a second level of indents for the sub-menu items, *For Ouput* and *For Input*. Finish by adding the *Exit* menu items.

Click **OK** to close the Menu Editor and return to Form Design. You will find that your form now has a menu bar. If you check the Objects list in the Properties window, you will also find that you now have another dozen controls.

Adding code to menu controls

Code can be added to any of the controls that are items on a pull-down menu, but *not* to those that figure in the menu bar. These controls only respond to a Click event, as all you ever do to a menu option is click on it.

Select the control to which you want to add code by clicking on its header in the menu bar then double-clicking on its caption when the menu drops down. The standard code window opens.

For example, if you click on the *Exit* name, then double-click on *Yes*, you should get to the **mnuExitYes_Click** procedure (or whatever you called it). Type in some code along these lines:

```
Private Sub mnuExitYes_Click ()
    Dim reply
```

```
        reply = MsgBox("Really exit ", 36, "Exit")
        If reply = 6 Then End
    End Sub
```

If you have worked through this example, save it – it could be useful later.

5.8 Worked example

This is an arithmetic test program, where the type and difficulty of the problems can be set by the user. The controls include a ScrollBar, a set of OptionButtons and a Menu, as well as others covered in earlier chapters. In its code you will find a **Select Case** and a variety of **If** structures.

- Another point to note here is how the values held by some of the controls are treated as variables.

It is not possible to draw a straightforward JSP design for the program as the operations are split among the procedures attached to controls, and the flow of execution is largely dependent on the user's interaction with the controls.

The best approach with this, as with most Visual Basic programs, is to start with the form design and to look at the actions that arise from the use of the controls.

Form design

For this program we want a form that will display an arithmetic problem and accept and check an answer. It should have a means of changing the type of problem and the level of difficulty, and should display the score. A possible layout is shown below.

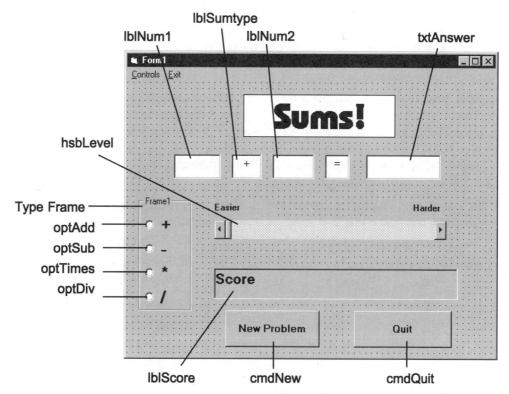

Figure 5.6 The form design – unnamed controls are purely decorative.

Controls and Events

lblNum1 and **lblNum2** are Labels that will hold numbers generated at random.

lblSumtype is a Label that holds the symbol for the type of sum.

txtAnswer is a Text Box – the only control into which the user can type. It will need code attached to its KeyPress event to check the answer when [Enter] is pressed.

The **Type** Frame contains four OptionButtonss, named **optAdd, optSub, optTimes** and **optDiv**. Code attached to their Click events will change *lblSumtype*'s Caption, and therefore its Value.

hsbLevel is a Horizontal Scroll Bar that sets the level of difficulty. When a new problem is generated, its value will be used to determine the scale of the numbers in expressions like:

        Num1 = Int(Rnd * hsbLevel) + 1

Its limits are fixed by the Min and Max Properties which are set at design time. If the program is intended for use by young children, the limits might be set at 5 and 10; for older users, armed with calculators, they might be 10 to 100 or more. As the value of *Level* is being used directly in this program, no code is needed to handle this control.

lblScore is a Label to display the current score. This will be updated by the checking routine attached to *txtAnswer*. To keep the score, we will need variables to count the number of goes and of correct answers. They must be set up in the general declarations.

cmdNew is a Command Button. When clicked, its code will generate a new problem and calculate the correct answer. As this value will be needed by the answer-checking routine, it must be held in a variable declared at the general level.

cmdQuit is a Command Button. Its code may be no more than the word '*End*', but can be improved by the use of a MsgBox to confirm that the user really wants to quit.

Random numbers

The **Rnd** function produces a fractional value in the range of 0 to 1. It is a pseudo-random – i.e. every value is as likely as every other, and you cannot predict what will come next, but it is actually the result of a complex calculation. Values such as 0.4162738746 are rarely much use in a program, but they can easily be converted into more useful ones by expressions following this pattern:

        num = Int(Rnd * range) + base

If you want numbers in the range 1 to 6, for a Dice simulator, the line would be:

        num = Int(Rnd * 6) + 1

The *base* number is necessary as **Int** truncates values – it chops off the decimal part, leaving just the integer. Look what happens with these values:

Rnd	Rnd * 6	Int(Rnd * 6)	Int(Rnd * 6) + 1
0.54	3.24	3	4
0.05	0.3	0	1
0.9	5.4	5	6

The calculation that produces random numbers always works through the same sequence. This sequence is so massive that you cannot predict the next number, as long as you start at a different place each time.

To make the system do this, place this statement near the top of your code:

Randomize

That selects a new start point, based on the system's clock.

Menu commands

These replicate the effects of the controls on the form. Though this is unnecessary, you will often find similar situations in Windows application programs. It takes very little code to offer menu, keystroke and icon or button alternatives to activate the same command, but it does give your users the choice. Some people like to pick their way through menus, others prefer a quick click on the screen. We are using menus and buttons here to give practice in both.

The menu structure is:

Menu Option	Comment
Controls	Header
New Problem	= cmdNew_Click
Type of Sum	
Add	= optAdd_Click
Subtract	= optSub_Click
Times	= optTimes_Click
Divide	= optDiv_Click
Exit	Header
Yes	= cmdQuit_Click
No	does nothing

The menu could well be added after the main program is up and running.

Coding

Much of the code flows naturally from the specifications of the controls, with a little more detailed design needed for a couple of larger routines.

```
general declarations
    Dim Ans As Single           ' the correct answer
    Dim rtans As Integer,        ' right answers
    Dim qcount As Integer        ' count of questions
Private Sub form_load ()
    Randomize
    qcount = 0                   ' count of questions
    rtans = 0                    ' score of correct answers
    lblSumtype = "+"             ' default type of sum
    hsbLevel = 10                ' degree of difficulty
End Sub
```

Generating a new problem

This procedure, run from the *cmdNew*, takes the shape:

```
Generate two random numbers
store them in lblNum1 & lblNum2
Work out the correct answer, storing it in the variable Ans
```

> The calculation to vary according to the character in lblSumtype
> Clear txtAnswer and place the cursor there ready for the response

Storing number values in Labels creates a problem when you start to calculate with them. Values in Labels are of the data type *Variant*. Visual Basic handles this intelligently, treating the values as numbers where you are obviously using them as numbers, and as strings where you are obviously using them as strings. The problem comes from the fact that there is one operator – the + sign – which can be used with both numbers and strings! It can be used to add two numbers, or to join two strings into a longer one.

> **9 + 9 = 18   but   "9" + "9" = "99"**

You can perform subtraction, multiplication or division by simple expressions such as:

> **Ans = lblNum1 – lblNum2**

But if you want to add, you must make the system get the number value from the Label with the **Val** function:

> **Ans = Val(lblNum1) + Val(lblNum2)**

(Using **Val**() on the first alone is enough to let Basic know that you want a number.)

```
Private Sub cmdNew_Click ()
    lblNum1 = Int(Rnd * hsbLevel) + 1          ' generate a random number
    lblNum2 = Int(Rnd * hsbLevel) + 1

    Select Case lblSumtype                     ' neater than a set of Ifs
        Case "+"
            Ans = Val(lblNum1) + Val(lblNum2)
        Case "-"
            Ans = lblNum1 – lblNum2
        Case "*"
            Ans = lblNum1 * lblNum2
        Case "/"
            Ans = lblNum1 / lblNum2
    End Select
    txtAnswer = ""                             ' clear the Answer box
    txtAnswer.SetFocus                         ' moves the cursor into it
End Sub
```

We can run this same code from the menu by making the menu selection call up the button's Click event:

```
Private Sub mnuNew_Click()
    cmdNew_Click
End Sub
```

Answer checking

The answer must be checked. We could ask our user to click on a Check button, but it will probably be simpler – for the user – if we look for the [Enter] key press that will tell us he or she has finished typing the answer.

We can spot this with the *KeyPress* event which has a *KeyAscii* parameter, giving the Ascii code of the last key that was pressed. Dig out your Ascii tables, and you can check for any character you like. [Enter] is Ascii 13.

The design of the rest of this routine is straightforward:

```
if  Enter is pressed
      get the value from the answer box
      if the answer is correct
            increase the score
      else display the correct answer
      increase the question count
      display the current score and count
```

In the correct answer and the score display we can use either + or & as a concatenator to join the variables and the accompanying text. It is not necessary to convert the numbers to strings first.

"The correct answer was " & Ans

You must leave a space after &. If you do not, the system will assume that '&Ans' is a name and there will be nothing to join it to the preceding text.

```
Private Sub txtAnswer_KeyPress (KeyAscii As Integer)
   If keyascii = 13 Then
      a = Val(txtAnswer)                          ' get the number value
      If a = Ans Then
         MsgBox "Correct"
         rtans = rtans + 1
      Else
         MsgBox "The answer was" & Ans, 48        ' with an info symbol
      End If
      qcount = qcount + 1
      lblScores.Caption = "Score = " & rtans & " out of " & qcount
   End If
End Sub
```

Changing the Sumtype

When the *lblSumtype* is changed via the Options, we can to set its new value directly:

```
Private Sub optAdd_Click ()
   lblSumtype = "+"
End Sub
```

The other options buttons have almost identical code.

When it is changed via the menu, we only need to set the Option. This invokes the Option's Click event, and therefore sets the *Sumtype* value:

```
Sub mnuAdd_Click ()
   AddOpt = True
End Sub
```

Extensions to the basic design

Add a button or menu item to allow the user to reset the score.

At any Level setting, the multiplications and divisions will be much harder than the additions or subtractions. How could you make them easier?

How could you ensure that the division problems always had a simple integer result?

5.9 Exercises

1. Design and write a program that could be used for the analysis of a simple questionnaire. This should only ask a single question, with a fixed set of possible answers – something along the lines of "What do you think of the canteen food? (A) Great value for money, (B) Good, (C) Fair, (D) Poor, (E) I'd rather starve."

   Use a set of Options and buttons marked *Next*, *Display Totals* and *Quit*. When the *Next* button is clicked, your code should scan the Options, add 1 to the appropriate total and clear the Options ready for the next response. Display Totals should produce a display of the question and the scores of the replies.

2. Design and write a program that will allow the user to type in text and to set its Bold, Italic and Underline properties using Check boxes.

Hint: The code in the Check Boxes could follow this pattern:

```
If chkBold Then
    Text1.FontBold = True
....
```

---

3. Take the menu structure developed above and add suitable code to each of the controls to give a simple demonstration of Options, Check boxes, InputBoxes, MsgBoxes. A demonstration for Menus will not be needed, as the program is one in itself, but you should at least have a comment or message appearing on the screen.

Hint: To keep the screen display clean and simple at runtime, turn off the Visible property of the Frames, Labels and other controls that you will use in your various demonstrations. It can then be turned back on when a particular demonstration is selected, and off when it ends.

A possible solution to Exercise 2 is given in Appendix A; solutions to Exercise 1 and 3 are included in the Lecturer's Supplement disk.

The files for the *Sums* program are available from the Visual Basic page at the author's Web site: http://www.tcp.co.uk/~macbride

6 Testing and debugging

6.1 Errors and error spotting

Visual Basic is a tried and tested product. Any errors in your code are entirely yours! Fortunately, the system provides some excellent tools for finding and correcting errors. There are two categories of error.

- **Syntax errors** are mistakes in the way that the language is used – typically spelling key words wrongly, trying to give the wrong type of data to a function, or missing out an essential part of a structure. These are usually spotted by the system, either at code-writing stage or when it compiles the program at the start of a run. Those caused by using the wrong data types for variables or with functions may not show up until the lines are executed.

- **Logical errors** occur when you use the words and structures correctly, but don't quite manage to say what you mean. Visual Basic has no means of identifying these, and unless the error crashes the program or produces visibly strange results, you may not even be aware of them yourself. Professional software developers, including MicroSoft, have been known to release programs with bugs that only showed up when the programs were pushed to their limits by users. To ensure that you have found and cured all logical errors, you must design a thorough testing procedure that will explore every possible route through the program, and every possible combination of values. Any problems thrown up by the testing can be then investigated using the debugging tools.

Scanning for errors

When you are writing your code, as soon as you press [Enter] at the end of the line, or move the cursor off, the line is scanned for errors. If one is found, it will be reported in a message box. The meaning is usually obvious, and will point out missing keywords, brackets, or other punctuation. Sometimes it is not so obvious. For example, while writing a startup password procedure I got this message:

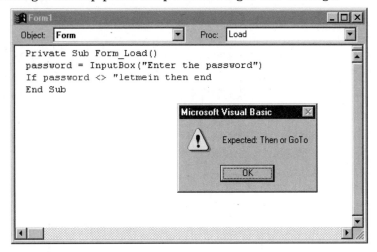

Figure 6.1 Error messages are usually good guides – but not always.

There is clearly a **Then** in the line. So what is the problem? Look to the left and you will see that the end quotes are missing around the password text. As far as the system is concerned, everything that follows the opening quote is text. Always check quotes if you get strange error messages.

If no errors are found, the line is rewritten in a standard format. Spaces are inserted around symbols, and those words that the system recognises as being part of the Visual Basic vocabulary are forced into mixed upper and lower case and recoloured. Do check the revised line. A misspelt keyword will occasionally fail to produce an error message, because the system assumes you means something entirely different. If you find that a word has not been reformatted, first check its spelling, then check your quotes. One or other will almost certainly be the cause of the problem.

Compile-time error reports

Though the line scan will pick up errors on individual lines, it cannot check the syntax of **If**, **Case**, **Loop** or similar structures that spread over several lines. If you begin program execution with a **Start** command, or the 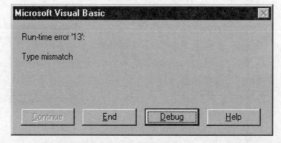, the errors will be picked up when the program reaches the code containing them. Begin with a **Start with Full Compile** command, and they will be spotted during the attempt to compile the code. In both cases, the system will display an error message and highlight the line which it believes to be the cause of the error. Though usually right, the system is not infallible. Complex **If** structures or sets of nested **Loops** can leave the system almost as confused as their authors. You will find it easier to sort out these problems if you indent your structures consistently. (See Chapter 4.)

Runtime error reports

There are some errors that will slip through these nets, but bring the program crashing to a halt at some point during its execution. Typically these errors revolve around data types – the data that you are attempting to pass from one variable, function or control to another is of the wrong type for its target. A second common cause is attempting to use a control, a file or other object which doesn't exist. You may have misspelt the name, or changed it, or deleted the object during an earlier edit.

This time the error is displayed in a message box, offering you the options to **Debug** or **End** the program. **End** simply closes down the program, and opens the code window at the point where you were last working – which may or may not be helpful. **Debug** will open the Debug window and highlight the error.

You will find it easier to deal with these kind of errors if you have a list of the controls and variables (and their types). A moment's reference to the list can save an hour's head-scratching and hunting through the code. Being organised really does work!

6.2 Debugging tools

The best debugging tools are a piece of paper and a pencil. Use these to design your program, to write up your list of variables and to dry run the design. Use them thoroughly and you won't have (m)any bugs, or much need for Visual Basic's debugging tools. But before we turn to those, have a look at the Debug window.

Breaking and entering

If you are getting peculiar results on screen and cannot understand where they are coming from, break into the program. The **Run | Break** command, the ❚❚ icon and **[Ctrl]-[Break]** will all suspend the program and open the Debug window.

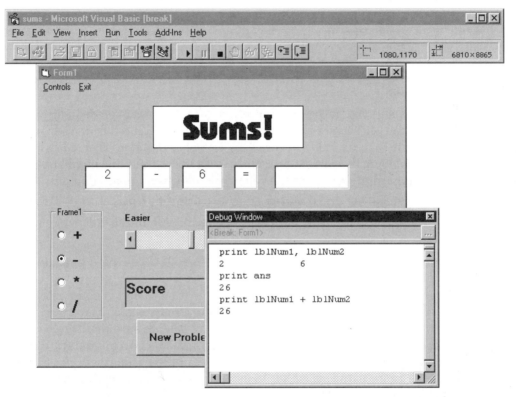

Figure 6.2 The Debug window can show what's happening beneath the surface.

You can use the *Print* command directly in the Debug window to display the values held by suspect variables. For example, while implementing the Sums program from the last chapter, you might find that addition gives strange results, with sums like 2 + 6 = 8 being marked wrong. Why is that? If you have added a message box to show the right answer, you may see why immediately. If not, breaking in and printing the values of *lblNum1*, *lblNum2* and *Ans* should lead you to the source of the error.

The Debug window will do more than display the values held in variables. You can also use it to test out many operations in immediate mode, i.e. performing them directly in that window. In this case, the problem lies in the '*lbNum1* + *lbNum2*' expression that produces the value of *Ans*. A **Watch** will help us to solve that problem (see below).

Bump starting

The Debug window can also be used to assign values to variables and properties to controls, so that you can simulate particular conditions during testing.

Assign the values or properties as you would do in your normal code:

```
sumtype = "+"
doneLooping = False
Text1.Text = "This is a test"
```

Restart the program with the ▶ icon or **Run | Continue**. The flow will pick up from where you left off.

Note: You can also restart the program at a Procedure, by typing its name in the Debug window.

6.3 Breakpoints

Breakpoints allow you to bring a program to a halt at a predefined point in a procedure. When you set a breakpoint in a line of code and run the program, execution will halt and the Debug window opens when it reaches that line. The Code window will also open, displaying the current procedure, with the current line highlighted. You do not get this immediate access to the relevant code if you break in directly.

Breakpoints can be set – and removed – during editing, by **Run | Toggle Breakpoint** or with the 🖑 icon. The relevant line will be recoloured in the code window to show that a breakpoint is present.

Any number of breakpoints may be set, and **Run | Clear All Breakpoints** will remove them all at once when the bugs have been ironed out. In practice you would rarely want more than two or three breakpoints at once, as too many interruptions make it difficult to follow the flow of the program. Use Breakpoints to track down one bug at a time, placing one at the last point where you are sure that the code is good, and another further on. After running the program and checking the state of crucial variables when each breakpoint is reached, you can then bring them closer together, repeating the process until you have identified the troublesome block or line of code.

6.4 Keeping watch

The two Watch facilities will track the values of variables, the properties of controls or the results of calcuated expressions.

Both **Instant Watch** and **Add Watch** allow you to set up a Watch expression which can be linked to a Breakpoint. **Add Watch** is the simplest to use. Call it up during editing, or after a **Break**, using the command on the Tools menu.

- If your interest is in what is going into a variable or control, type its name as the Expression; set the Context – typically a selected procedure for a variable and the Form for a control; and set the Watch Type as **Break when Expression has Changed**.
- If you want to watch out for a variable or control holding a particular value, or going beyond a limit, type a logical test, such as $X = 1000$ or $Num < MaxNum$

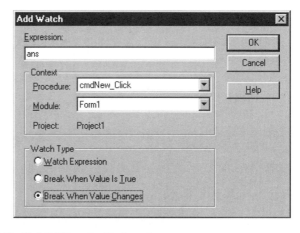

Figure 6.3 The Edit/Add Watch dialog box.

The simplest and most effective way to use a Watch is to set a Breakpoint When Value Changes (or is True), and place it in the Context of a Procedure.

for the Expression; select the procedure in which this could occur as the Context; and set the Watch Type as **Break when Expression is True**.

- When the program is run, or restarted, the system will keep a watch on the expression and break execution when the conditions are met. The code window will open, with the current line highlighted. The Debug window will also be open, and will show, in its upper pane, the current value of the variable, or expression.

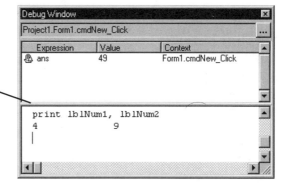

The upper pane remains open after all Watches have been removed. To close it, drag the dividing bar up to the top.

Figure 6.4 The Debug window with a Watch set.

Instant Watch offers an alternative to typing in the Debug window if you want to see the value of a variable or an expression.

- Go into Break mode, either from reaching a breakpoint or by interrupting the program directly. If necessary, open the Code window and select the procedure that you are interested in.
- Select the variable, control name or expression to check and click the 🔍 icon or select **Instant Watch** from the **Tools** or the short menu.
- The **Instant Watch** dialog box will open, displaying the current value of the selected variable or expression.

Tip:	**Instant Watch** can be used to set up new Watch expressions, but is not recommended – it is simpler to start from **Add Watch**.

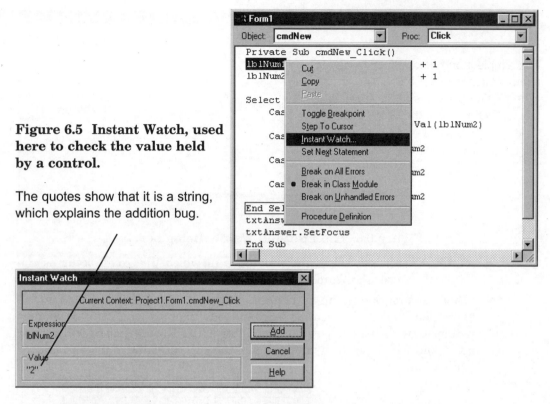

Figure 6.5 Instant Watch, used here to check the value held by a control.

The quotes show that it is a string, which explains the addition bug.

6.5 Stepping through

Sometimes the best way to see what is happening in a program is slow it down to a speed at which you can follow it. For this we have the Step commands. They can be used as a way of starting execution, or restarting after a break.

- **Tools | Step Into** or the ⬚ icon will execute one line at a time, allowing you to use the Debug window or Instant Watch to check the progress of variables as you go.
- **Tools | Step Over** or the ⬚ icon will execute a whole procedure, so that you can skip over the parts that you know function perfectly.

In Stepping, the code window opens, and the relevant line is highlighted as it is executed. As this will partially, or totally, obscure the active form, be prepared to switch between the two as you follow the action.

6.6 Error-trapping

In common with most other Basics, Visual Basic supports the **On Error** statement which can trap run-time errors. Use this to find the flaws in your logic and to guard against the program crashing when your users fail to behave themselves. It is particularly useful in filing operations, for it can pick up the 'File not found', 'Drive not ready' and other common – and fatal – mistakes that can occur when accessing drives.

Errors can only be trapped within a procedure, so if you have several places at which fatal errors are possible, each must have its own routine. The syntax takes the form:

```
Sub ....
    On Error GoTo labelled_line
    ...
Exit Sub

labelled_line:
    display error message or counteract problem
Resume label or Next
```

On Error must be at the start of the procedure, before the possible source of error. The *labelled_line* and handling-code will typically be at the end. To avoid running into this by mistake, you must either force an early end with **Exit Sub** (see Chapter 8), or use another **GoTo** to jump over it.

How you handle the error is entirely up to you. If the purpose of the routine is to pick up flaws in the design during debugging, then the most sensible thing to do is to display a message box telling you what the error is. This can be found from the two system variables **Err** and **Error**. **Err** gives the error code, not very meaningful by itself; but **Error** translates the code into a message.

```
On Error GoTo errmess:
...
errmess:
MsgBox "The problem is " & Error(Err)
...
```

Now at least you know what you have got to deal with. If the error message does not give you enough to go on, look up *Trappable Errors* in the Help system to get more details.

Some 'errors' can simply be ignored. As you will see in Chapter 15, if the user presses Cancel on a dialog box generated by the Common Dialog control, Visual Basic treats this as an error. In practice, this is not a problem, as your user simply wishes to abandon the operation. All you need here is a jump to the end of the procedure:

```
Private Sub cmdSave_Click()
    On Error GoTo cancelled
    CD1.ShowSave
    ... code to handle saving
    cancelled:
End Sub
```

If the routine is there to idiot-proof the final program, then it should identify the error and either give a user-friendly message or substitute a default value, before returning to the main code. In either case, the routine must include a **Resume** statement. This tells the computer where to restart the flow of execution.

```
Resume Next
```

will pick up from the line following the one that produced the error. If you are using this, you should first deal with the error – perhaps by substituting a default value for the one your user failed to supply. In many cases, the error will have occurred when getting a filename or other value from the user, and the procedure will not be able to continue without a valid input. Here the best solution is to tell your user what the problem is, then Resume at a label placed past the relevant lines or at the end of the procedure. For example.

```
Private Sub Form_Click ()
    On Error GoTo errorsub
    number = InputBox("How many lines do I have to write?")
    For n = 1 To number
        Print "I must not make mistakes"
    Next n
Exit Sub

errorsub:
    MsgBox " Please enter a number when asked"
    Resume endline
endline:
End Sub
```

Task 6.1   Type the last example into the **Click** procedure of a form. Run the program and click. When asked for a number, try typing in a letter and see what happens. Edit the program and turn all the error-handling lines into comments by placing a single quote at the start. Run and click again, and see what happens this time when you fail to provide a number.

---

7 Graphics (1)

7.1 Objects and properties for drawing

Drawn graphics play a smaller part in this language than they do in others. Visual Basic provides very simple means to import and display images from graphics packages. Its Label and Text Box controls have Border and Color properties to enhance their appearance, so you do not need to create box outlines for them. It has a Shape control that will produce rectangles, circles and ovals in a variety of styles and the usual full range of colours. With these at hand, the need for fancy drawing facilities is much reduced. Nevertheless, there are three methods, **Pset**, **Line** and **Circle**, which will plot points of colour, draw lines and boxes, circles, ovals and arcs. They are worth exploring.

You can draw on a Form, a PictureBox or a Printer object, and on no others. The basic appearance of the graphic is determined by the properties of the object, though some aspects – principally colour – can also be specified in the drawing command.

ScaleMode

This defines the unit of measurement. The default is mode 1, **Twip**, a remarkably named and remarkably small unit. A Twip is a twentieth of a printer's Point – which makes the letters in this text 200 Twips high. Its advantages are that it is largely machine independent, ensuring that images translate well from screen to printer – and it does allow very accurate positioning.

ScaleMode 2 is the **Point** – the printer's measurement. With 72 points to the inch, this is also a very small unit. As fonts are measured in points, this Scalemode comes into its own when you are dealing largely with text.

ScaleMode 3, **Pixel**, is screen-based, and varies with machines. The size of pixels that you see depends upon the resolution of your monitor.

Other possible modes will give you measurements in characters, inches, millimetres and centimetres.

DrawMode

This affects how the drawn line interacts with the background. There are 16 modes to choose from, but the two most useful are mode 13, *Copy Pen*, which overwrites anything in the background in the chosen foreground colour; and mode 7, *Xor Pen*. In this mode, colours are distorted when overwriting other colours, but if the same line is drawn twice, it removes the first line, restoring the previous image.

BackColor, FillColor and ForeColor

The *BackColor* applies to the whole Form or PictureBox. Any existing drawings will be erased if you change it during the program's execution.

The *FillColor* refers to the lines which will appear in a box or circle if you have chosen a patterned *FillStyle*. The *ForeColor* determines the colour of the outlines. All of these can be changed at runtime and will only affect subsequent drawings – existing ones remaining in their original style and colour. Outline colour can be changed more conveniently within the drawing commands.

DrawStyle

This can be 0, *Solid* or 5, *Transparent*, or one or other Dash and Dot combinations in between. These are only available with lines of DrawWidth 1, not thicker ones.

DrawWidth

This sets the width of the drawn (outside) lines only, and has no effect on the FillStyle line, if present. The width setting is always in pixels, whatever the ScaleMode unit.

FillStyle

This refers to the pattern to be drawn in a closed rectangle or circle. The key modes are 0, *Solid*, in which the drawn shape is filled with the FillColor, and 1, *Transparent*. Modes 2 and on, produce hatching with thin lines of FillColor.

There are exercises at the end of this chapter which will create programs to explore the effect of Property settings on drawn graphics.

7.2 Lines

The Line method can draw points, lines, open and filled rectangles. Its syntax is:

Line Step (*xStart,yStart*) - [Step] (*xEnd,yEnd*), *PenColour*, BF

Everything, apart from **Line** - *(xEnd,yEnd)*, is optional.

Step makes the co-ordinates relative to the position defined by CurrentX, CurrentY, the system variables that record the last point plotted. If omitted, the co-ordinates refer to the underlying object, with 0,0 at the top left.

(xStart,yStart), if omitted, starts the line from the CurrentX,CurrentY position.

PenColour sets the colour of the line, using either the RGB or the QBColor function. (See page 75.) If omitted, the control's ForeColor property will be used instead.

B stands for Block, and will produce a rectangle.

F stands for Fill, and will fill the rectangle with the *PenColour*, or ForeColor.

If you want to use the B or F options without setting the *PenColour*, you must place an extra comma to hold the space where the colour value would have been.

The examples in Figure 7.1 were produced by the commands:

1   **Line -(2000, 500)**

When first run, the CurrentX and CurrentY values are both 0. If this command is given again, the line will have a different start point.

2   **colour = RGB(255, 0, 40)**   'red with a dash of green
    Line (1000, 1000)-(6000, 1000), colour

Here both ends and the colour have been defined.

3   **colour = QBColor(4)**   'deep blue
    Line (1000, 2000)-(3000, 4000), colour, B

This uses the B option to create an open block. Its central area is hatched by the Form's FillStyle setting.

4   **Line (4000, 3000)-(6000, 5000), , BF**

Here the BF option produces a solid block of colour. Notice the extra comma to mark the place where the colour option would have gone.

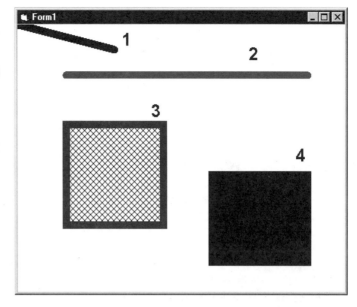

Figure 7.1 Four images drawn by versions of the Line command.

Notice that lines have rounded ends, though the rectangles have sharp corners.

The DrawWidth was set to 10, the FillStyle to 7 – Diagonal Cross.

7.3 Circle

The options here will allow you to draw arcs, segments and ovals as well as circles. The syntax is:

Circle Step (*x,y*), *radius, colour, start, end, aspect*

Only *Circle (x,y), radius* is essential.

Step and *Colour* are the same as for Line.

Start and *end* set the limits of the arc. Angles are given in radians, working anti-clockwise from 0 (due East), and with 2*Pi radians in a full circle. If written as a negative, the angle is converted back to positive, but a line is drawn from the centre to the arc. If both start and end are given as negatives, the arc becomes a segment, and will be filled in the FillStyle, FillColor settings.

Aspect sets the aspect ratio, i.e. the relative height and width of the shape. A value less than 1 produces a flattened ellipse; more than 1 produces a narrow ellipse.

If any arguments are omitted, their places must be held by commas.

The examples in Figure 7.2 were drawn by:

   1 Circle (1000, 1000), 500

The basic circle, filled as the FillStyle is set to 0 – Solid.

   2 Circle (4000, 2000), 1000, , 1, 3

An arc stretching from 1 to 3 radians.

   3 Circle (1500, 3000), 1000, , , , 0.5

Here the 0.5 aspect value flattens the shape into an ellipse.

   4 Circle (4000, 3000), 1000, , -0.5, -4

The arc here runs from 0.5 to 4 radians, but the minus signs cause lines to be drawn from the centre to the ends of the arc, creating a segment.

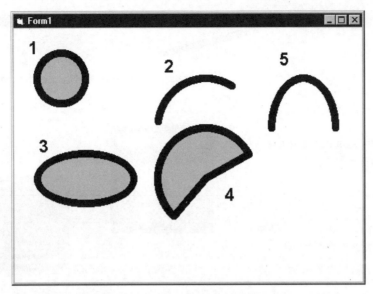

Figure 7.2 Five shapes drawn with versions of the Circle command.

5   Circle (6000, 2000), 1000, , , 3.14, 1.5

This elliptical arc starts at the default of 0 and runs half way round. (3.14 is near enough to Pi at this resolution.)

7.4 Pset

This is the last of the drawing methods. It plots a point of colour, the size of the point being determined by the DrawWidth. Try this example to see it at work.

This **Form_Click** procedure produces randomly coloured points at random places on the form. The **DblClick** stops the process by setting the variable *stopit* to True. *stopit* must be set up in **general declarations**.

```
Private Sub Form_Click ()
    stopit = False
    Do
        red = Rnd * 255
        green = Rnd * 255
        blue = Rnd * 255
        x = Rnd * 8000
        y = Rnd * 8000
        PSet (x, y), RGB(red, green, blue)
        DoEvents                    ' essential for the Double-Click to be picked up
    Loop Until stopit
End Sub

Private Sub Form_DblClick ()
    stopit = True
End Sub
```

If you are mathematically inclined, you may like to explore the possibilities of plotting lines and curves using Pset. By keeping the DrawWidth low and plotting close together, you can produce very smooth lines.

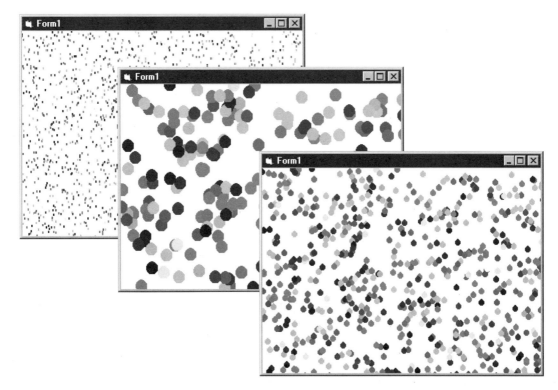

Figure 7.3 The Pset test program with DrawWidths of 2, 8 and 16.

7.5 RGB and QBColor

In Visual Basic, colours are always held by long integers of the type &H008080FF& – you see examples of these every time you pick a Property colour from the palette. They are not nice numbers to handle. You can always copy a colour number out of the property window and paste it into your code, but there are also two other ways to set colours which you may find easier to handle.

In the **RGB** function, the colour is defined by values for Red, Green and Blue. Each of these will be between 0 and 255, giving you a theoretical range of 256^3 (16+ million) colours. In practice, the Line and Circle functions seem to work with a restricted set of 16 colours, though a larger palette is available for filled areas.

You can use the function directly as an argument to the drawing method, to set the colour of that object only:

```
Line (1000,1000) – (2000, 1000), RGB(255,0,0)
```

or pass it to a variable – a good approach if you want to use the same colour several times in the program:

```
red= RGB(255,0,0)
Line (1000,1000) – (2000, 1000), red
```

or use it to set a Property – so that all subsequent drawings are that colour:

```
ForeColor = RGB(255, 0, 0)
Line (1000,1000) – (2000, 1000)
```

These will all draw a line of 1000 points in bright red.

The **QBColor** function converts the 0 to 15 colour palette used by QBasic and many other languages, into an RGB colour value. The codes are given here for interest. In practice you can simply let the system get on with the conversion without worrying about it.

QBCode	Colour	RGB	QBCode	Colour	RGB
0	Black	0,0,0	8	Grey	128,128,128
1	Blue	128,0,0	9	Light Blue	255,0,0
2	Green	0,128,0	10	Light Green	0,255,0
3	Cyan	128,128,0	11	Light Cyan	255,255,0
4	Red	0,0,128	12	Light Red	0,0,255
5	Magenta	128,0,128	13	Light Magenta	255,0,255
6	Brown	0,128,128	14	Yellow	0,255,255
7	White	128,128,128	15	Bright White	255,255,255

What is the binary pattern behind the QBColor codes?

Task 7.1	Write a program that loops through the QBColor codes, drawing a thick line of each colour. The lines should be horizontal and about 200 Twips apart.

7.6 The amateur painter

The following example program puts the Line and Circle methods to work, to create a Paint-style drawing program. It lacks many of the finer touches of even that simple graphics package, but it demonstrates some of the core techniques for using the drawing methods.

The basic plan is to set up a PictureBox to use as a canvas, with buttons to select the drawing tools, and sliders to control the DrawWith and the colour. The selection controls can all be laid out around the canvas, giving a clear and simple user interface. That leads us to the form design shown below.

Form design

The button controls will set the variable that controls the drawing mode, and the FillStyle for the filled or open box and circle. The modes will be 1 – Freehand Drawing, 2 – Line, 3 – Box and Block, 4 – Circle and Round.

The bulk of the code in this program will handle the interaction of the mouse and the canvas. Lines, boxes and circles will be defined here, as in other Windows programs, by dragging an outline, with this turning into the finished image when the mouse button is released. We therefore have three events to handle: the *MouseDown*, at which initial values will be set or recorded; *MouseMove*, which will remove any existing outline and draw a new one; *MouseUp*, when the final shape will be drawn.

Freehand drawing is rather different. There is no simple way to do this on a temporary basis, so here the *MouseMove* will place the final image directly onto the canvas. We could use Pset for the Freehand drawing, but the system cannot pick up the mouse movements fast enough to create a solid line of Pset points, unless they are very large or you move the mouse very slowly.

The buttons should all be named after their captions; the scroll bars named after their colours.

The colour labels are there for clarity only.

The block to the left of the scroll bars is a Label – its BackColor will show the current colour.

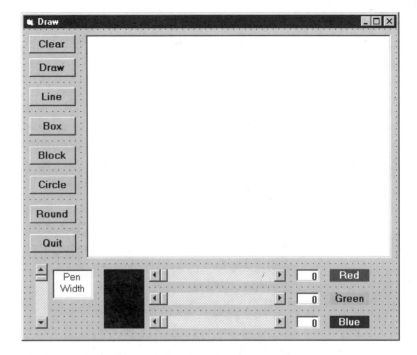

Figure 7.4 A possible layout for the Draw program.

A better solution will be to take advantage of the way that the Line method links back to the previously plotted point. This will also produce much smoother lines.

The colour ScrollBars will hold the values for red, green and blue, and combine them to update the pen colour, held in a *general* variable. An 'inkpot' to the side of the bars will display the current colour. Note that this colour will only apply properly to the filled shapes. Lines and outlines will appear in colours from the 16-colour palette.

Form implementation

The default Form is too small to give you a decent drawing area, so the first job is to make it larger. Next, place on the form:

- a **PictureBox** to cover the greater part of the form, and named *picCanvas*.
- eight **Command buttons** down the left side, named after the captions as shown in Figure 7.4, e.g. *cmbBlock*
- three **Horizontal ScrollBars** across the bottom, named *hsbRed*, *hsbGreen* and *hsbBlue*. Set their Properties: Min = 0, Max = 255; SmallChange = 1; LargeChange = 32 or 16.
- three **Labels** named *lblRedVal*, *lblGreenVal* and *lblBlueVal*, beside the bars, to display the current colour values. They should have their Back or ForeColors set appropriately, and be captioned with 0 – the initial colour settings. You may also want to add named Labels beside them, as in Figure 7.4.
- a **Label**, to the left of the ScrollBars. This will display the current ForeColor, produced from the RGB function and the ScrollBar values. Name it *lblInkpot*.
- a **Vertical ScrollBar** in the bottom left, named *vsbPenWidth*. A Label to display its value could be added if wanted.

7.7 Code design

The routines that handle the drawing must be properly planned. In the process, we can identify the variables that will be needed.

There are three event procedures for the mouse as it interacts with the canvas – *MouseDown*, *MouseMove* and *MouseUp*. All have arguments that will tell you which button is down, the state of the [Shift] and [Ctrl] keys, and the current position of the mouse. Between them they can handle starting to draw, drawing, and erasing the temporary lines and drawing the final image. The intermediate stage is crucial, and is our startpoint.

picCanvas_MouseMove

We could use a JSP diagram for this, or write the design in pseudo-code. The latter may show the branching clearer than a JSP diagram. Variables are picked out in italics.

This should only be performed if the button is down.

1   If the *mode* is set for any kind of line, then
      if there is an existing copy
          redraw it to erase it
      draw a new copy
2   If the *mode* is set for any kind of circle, then
      if there is an existing copy
          redraw it to erase it
      calculate the new radius
      draw a new copy
3   If the *mode* is Freehand drawing, then
      if there is a drawn point already
          draw a line from it to the current point
      otherwise
          draw a line from the start to the current point
4   Store the *Xold,Yold* values for use next time
5   Set the variable *started* to 1, to indicate that the drawing process has started

picCanvas_MouseDown

1   Sets the properties of the canvas to suit the drawing mode. Apart from the Freehand drawing, all images will initially be shown in thin dashed lines.

Property	Freehand draw	All Others
DrawMode	13 – Copy Pen	7 – Xor, so that overdrawing erases
DrawStyle	0 – Solid	1 – Dashed
DrawWidth	PenWidth	1 pixel
FillStyle	N/A	1 – Transparent

2   Pick up the mouse's current X and Y positions, from the X,Y parameters of this procedure, and store them in Xstart and Ystart. They are the start position for lines and boxes, and the centre of a circle.

picCanvas_MouseUp

1 Set the Properties to produce solid lines, using the current ink colour, at the current *PenWidth* thickness. The FillStyle will depend upon the choice of Box or Block, Circle or Round. If it is held in a variable, *FS* , this could be set when the mode is selected.

2 Draw the object, using the appropriate Line or Circle method.

Selection Buttons

- All will set the *mode* variable.
- Box, Block, Circle and Round will set the *FS* (FillStyle) variable, with 0 – Solid or 1 – Transparent.
- Circle and Round will set the *radius* to 0.

7.8 Coding

Variables

The design has established the variables needed by the program. Their values are to be accessed by several controls and buttons, and they must therefore be declared in the general declarations area. Our coding can start here.

```
general declarations
    Dim xstart As Integer, ystart As Integer      ' start of line, centre of circle
    Dim xold As Integer, yold As Integer          ' old end of line
    Dim started As Integer                        ' flag that drawing has begun
    Dim rad As Integer                            ' radius of circle
    Dim ink As Long
    Dim mode As Integer
    Dim FS As Integer
```

We do not need variables for *PenWidth* or the *Red*, *Green*, *Blue* colour values, as these can be taken directly from the relevant controls.

```
Private Sub Form_Load ()
    mode = 0                          ' initialisation of key values
    ink = RGB(hsbRed, hsbGreen, hsbBlue)
    picCanvas.DrawWidth = 4
End Sub
Private Sub cmdClear_Click ()
    picCanvas.Cls                     ' clear the display
    mode = 0                          ' not drawing
End Sub
Private Sub cmdDraw_Click ()
    mode = 1                          ' select Freehand drawing
End Sub
Private Sub cmdLine_Click ()
    mode = 2
End Sub
```

```
Private Sub cmdBox_Click ()
    mode = 3
    FS = 1                              ' so that FillStyle can be Transparent
End Sub
Private Sub cmdBlock_Click ()
    mode = 3                            ' same mode as Box
    FS = 0                              ' but different FillStyle
End Sub
Private Sub cmdCircle_Click ()
    mode = 4
    rad = 0                             ' start with a 0 wide circle
    FS = 1                              ' not filled
End Sub
Private Sub cmdRound_Click ()
    mode = 4
    rad = 0
    FS = 0
End Sub
Private Sub hsbRed_Change ()
    ink = RGB(hsbRed, hsbGreen, hsbBlue)    ' uses new value to reset the ink
    lblRedVal = hsbRed                      ' and the number display
    lblInkpot.BackColor = ink               ' and the inkpot display
End Sub
```

hsbGreen_Change and **hsbBlue_Change** are virtually identical.

The **vsbPenWidth** ScrollBar needs no code unless you want to add a display on the same lines as that for the colours.

```
Private Sub picCanvas_MouseDown (Button As Integer, Shift As Integer, x As Single, y As Single)
    If mode = 1 Then                        'Properties for Freehand
        picCanvas.DrawMode = 13             'Copy pen
        picCanvas.DrawStyle = 0             ' Solid
        picCanvas.DrawWidth = vsbPenWidth
    Else                                    ' Properties for all others
        picCanvas.DrawMode = 7
        picCanvas.FillStyle = 1             ' Transparent
        picCanvas.DrawWidth = 1             ' thin
        picCanvas.DrawStyle = 1             ' Dash
        picCanvas.ForeColor = &HFF0000      ' any colour you like, really
    End If
    started = 0                             'not started yet
    xstart = x                              'x,y taken from the arguments
    ystart = y
    xold = x
    yold = y
End Sub
```

If mode<7| Else Then

x start & xold both= X
ystart & yold both = Y

X, Y taken from the arguments

```
Private Sub picCanvas_MouseMove (Button As Integer, Shift As Integer, x As
Single, y As Single)
    If Button <> 0 Then                              ' button is held down
        Select Case mode
        Case 1                                        ' Freehand
            If started Then
                picCanvas.Line -(x, y), ink          ' link to last point
            Else
                picCanvas.Line (xstart, ystart)-(x, y), ink    ' or start from scratch
            End If
        Case 2                                        'overwrite old
            If started Then picCanvas.Line (xstart, ystart)-(xold, yold)
                picCanvas.Line (xstart, ystart)-(x, y)        ' draw new one
        Case 3
            If started Then picCanvas.Line (xstart, ystart)-(xold, yold), , B
                picCanvas.Line (xstart, ystart)-(x, y), , B
        Case 4
            If started Then picCanvas.Circle (xstart, ystart), rad
            rad = Sqr((xstart – x) ^ 2 + (ystart – y) ^ 2)      ' Pythagorus
            picCanvas.Circle (xstart, ystart), rad
        End Select
        xold = x                                      ' store x,y for next time
        yold = y
        started = 1                                   ' we've started
    End If
End Sub
Private Sub picCanvas_MouseUp (Button As Integer, Shift As Integer, x As Single,
y As Single)
    picCanvas.FillStyle = FS                  'set Properties for final image
    picCanvas.FillColor = ink
    picCanvas.DrawMode = 13
    picCanvas.DrawWidth = vsbPenwidth
    picCanvas.DrawStyle = 0
    If Button = 1 And mode <>0 Then           'only if you are drawing
        Select Case mode
        Case 2
            picCanvas.Line (xstart, ystart)-(x, y), ink
        Case 3
            picCanvas.Line (xstart, ystart)-(x, y), ink, B
        Case 4
            picCanvas.Circle (xstart, ystart), rad, ink
        End Select
    End If
End Sub
```

Freehand Drawing

If xstart, ystart are omitted, the line starts from the current X, current Y pos".

7.9 Exercises

1. Write a program to demonstrate the effects of different DrawModes on overlapping lines and circles. It might use two buttons – one to clear the form and draw a background pattern; the second to select a DrawMode and draw an overlapping image.

2. Write a program to investigate the range of colours that can be used with the Line, Circle and Pset methods on your system.

3. Write a 'screen-saver' style program, that produces a constantly changing image. This might be done by displaying a drawn graphic, pausing briefly, then clearing the screen and redrawing the graphic in a different position, or by drawing a succesion of images that graually obliterate those beneath.

4. Design and write a program that will take a set of 10 numbers and convert them into a bar chart and/or pie chart display. For a decent bar chart, you must scale your values to make best use of the available space. Before drawing the bars, find the largest number in the set and use this and the height of the display area to work out a suitable scale factor.

Possible solutions to Exercises 1, 2 and 3 are given in Appendix A; a solution for Exercise 4 is included in the Lecturer's Supplement disk.

The files for the *Draw* program are available from the Visual Basic page at the author's Web site: http://www.tcp.co.uk/~macbride

8 Procedures, functions and forms

8.1 Procedures and functions

Procedures and functions, both off-the-peg and tailor-made, are central to Visual Basic. So far, all the procedures and functions that we have used have been those built into the system, or those written to handle Events from Controls. As you have seen, you can get a long way with those alone. However, there are times when you can produce a more readable and efficient program by writing procedures and functions of your own. Readability is improved because it is easier to make sense of small blocks of code that do specific jobs, that of long routines that perform a variety of operations. Efficiency is improved when you need to perform the same operation at several different places in the program. Writing a common piece of code into a procedure, and calling it from each point, can save a lot of time and effort.

Procedures

A procedure is a block of code that performs some kind of operation. Up until now you have probably only used procedures that are linked to events. Free-standing ones are used like methods – which are effectively the same. Think for a moment about what *MsgBox*, *Line*, *Circle* and *Cls* have in common. Any non-event procedure will share these features.

It will be executed when it is *called* from elsewhere in the program, and at the end of its run, the flow will pass back to the point from which it was called. Values may be passed to the procedure through *arguments*, and the procedure may pass changed values back to the code that called it, or leave them unchanged. *Cls* takes no arguments; *Line*, *Circle* and *MsgBox* take a variable number of arguments.

The essential nature of the procedure is defined in its first line. This takes the form:

Sub *name* ([ByVal/ByRef] *arg_1* **As Type,** [ByVal/ByRef] *arg_2* **As Type,...)**

The arguments are optional, though the brackets must be there, even if empty. If the Type definitions are omitted, the arguments will be taken as Variants. Variants are, of course, more flexible. Where the Types are specified, you can only pass data of the right type to the arguments.

The optional **ByVal** or **ByRef** affects what happens to any variables that are passed to the procedure by the calling code. If **ByVal** is used, only the value of the variable is passed to the procedure, and its original value is unchanged in the calling code. **ByRef** passes the variable itself the procedure, so changes made there are retained on return to the program. In practice, you can normally omit them both at this level of programming.

The end of a procedure is marked by **End Sub**. If necessary, an early exit from the procedure can be forced by the **Exit Sub** statement.

Functions

A function is a block of code that returns a value to calling code. They will almost always take arguments, as the main purpose of functions is to convert values from one form to another. Built-in functions that we have used so far include *Sin* and *Cos*, *RGB* and *QBColor*. They appear in the calling code as values being assigned to variables, or used in expressions, or displayed on screen.

The syntax of function definition is almost identical to that of a procedure:

Function *name* (*arguments*) **As Type**

If the Type definition is omitted, the function returns a Variant.

At some point in the function, there must be a line that copies the calculated value to the function name, for passing back to the calling code. It takes the shape:

name = **value**

8.2 Creating a procedure

As an example, we will create a procedure that will draw polygons – it could be a useful addition to the Line and Circle methods. The process starts, as in all coding, with the design. What is the procedure going to do, how will it do it, and what values will be passed to it?

Any regular polygon can be drawn inside a circle, with its vertices touching the circumference.

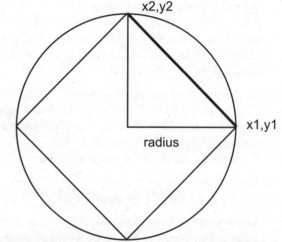

The x and y values of each vertex can be calculated from the angle and the radius.
Pairs of vertices can then be connected by the Line method.

Figure 8.1 Designing the polygon procedure.

The angle between one vertex and the next depends upon the number of sides and can be found by the formula:

internal_angle = (2 * Pi) / number_of_sides

where **2 * Pi** is the radian equivalent of 360 degrees.

We can loop through a full circle, in steps of *internal_angle* size, calculating the x,y co-ordinates of each vertex, and joining them with a line. To be able to draw the polygon, the procedure would need to be given the number of sides, the co-ordinates of the centre and the radius of the shape.

A procedure can be created from anywhere within the code window. Move the cursor below the **End Sub** of whatever procedure is there at present and type the first line:

Sub polygon (sides, x, y, radius)

As soon as you press [Enter], the line will be removed from that procedure and used to start a new procedure in the *general* area.

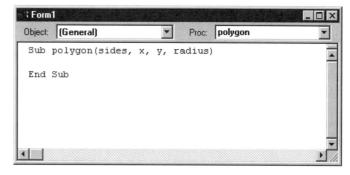

While it helps to get the definition line right from the start, you can alter and add to it later if necessary.

Figure 8.2 A new procedure, ready for its code.

The rest of the procedure can now be typed in.

Don't miss out the **CDdl()** (Convert to Double) functions in the fourth line. These convert the values, that were passed into the procedure as Variants, into numbers before they are added. If omitted, *x* and *radius* will be joined as strings! (In practice, you could omit one, for as long as at least one of the values is a number, + will produce a numeric result.)

Note that the loop through the *angle* value starts at *IntAng*, not 0. The x,y co-ordinates for that point are calculated from the *x, y* and *radius* values.

```
Sub polygon (sides, x, y, radius)
    Dim Pi As Double, Inc As Double
    Dim Xstart As Double, Ystart As Double, Xnext As Double, Ynext As Double
    Pi = 4 * Atn(1)                          'define Pi
    IntAng = 2 * Pi / sides                  'internal angle
    Xstart = CDbl(x) + CDbl(radius)          'convert Variants to Double
    Ystart = y
    For angle = IntAng To 2 * Pi Step IntAng
        Xnext = Cos(angle) * radius + x
        Ynext = Sin(angle) * radius + y
        Line (Xstart, Ystart)-(Xnext, Ynext)
        Xstart = Xnext                       'shuffle values for next line
        Ystart = Ynext
    Next angle
End Sub
```

To test the new procedure, attach suitable code to the *Form_Click* event. This may allow values to be input, as below, or used fixed values to create some demo shapes. Notice that when the procedure is called, its arguments are *not* enclosed in brackets.

```
Private Sub Form_Click ()
    Dim sides As Double, radius As Double, x As Double, y As Double
    sides = InputBox("Number of Sides")
    radius = InputBox("Radius")
    x = InputBox("X of centre")
    y = InputBox("Y of centre")
    polygon sides, x, y, radius
End Sub
```

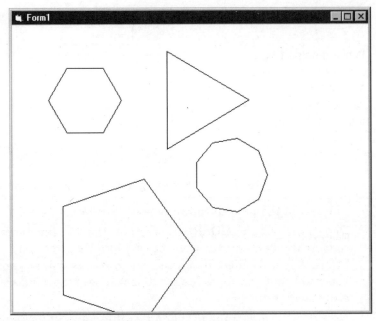

The InputBox will overlay and erase any existing lines. Set the Form's AutoDraw property to True so that the image is restored when the Form comes back into view.

Figure 8.3 The polygon procedure at work.

8.3 Creating a function

The process here is much the same as with a procedure, except that we must define the type of the returned value, and include a line that will return it. Try this example – especially if you dislike radians. It converts radians to degrees using the formula:

AngleInDegrees = AngleInRadians * 360 / 2 * Pi

This works because 360 degrees = 2 * Pi radians. If you prefer, the end part can be simplified to 180 / Pi.

```
Function degrees (rads As Double) As Double
    Dim Pi As Double
    Pi = 4 * Atn(1)
    degrees = rads * 180 / Pi          'pass the result out
End Function
```

The line beginning with the function name '**degrees = **' is crucial. This is the one that gets the result out of the function.

Write a suitable test routine that includes a line like this:

AngleInDegs = degrees(CDbl(AngleInRads))

Note that when calling functions, the arguments are enclosed in brackets.

(The **CDbl()** function will not be needed if *AngleInRads* is defined as a **Double**.)

Task 8.1   Write a function that will convert angles in degrees into radians. The formula is the reverse of the earlier one:

AngleInRadians = AngleInDegrees * Pi / 180

8.4 Recursive functions

A recursive function is one which calls itself. (As in the classic definition 'Recursion: see Recursion'.) This can be the most effective way to handle some kinds of mathematical operations. The two key points to remember when writing recursive functions are:

- somewhere there must be a line with the function name on both the left and the right sides of an = sign, which is where the function calls itself,
- somewhere else there must be a statement that passes a definite value to the function. This is the escape route. Without it, the function would call itself endlessly, until it crashed the system.

Factorials provide a clear, simple demonstration. A factorial is a number multiplied by every other whole number below it, down to 1, e.g.

Factorial 3 = 3 * 2 * 1

Factorial 4 = 4 * 3 * 2 * 1

Factorial 5 = 5 * 4 * 3 * 2 * 1

Think about it, and you will see that Factorial 5 could be found by 5 * Factorial 4; Factorial 4 by 4 * Factorial 3, and so on.

From this, we can derive the general rule:

Factorial n = n * Factorial (n-1)

As Factorial (1-1) is 0, the rule is different for 1:

Factorial 1 = 1

From these two rules we can define the function.

```
Function Factorial (num As Double) As Double
    If num = 1 Then
        Factorial = 1                          ' the escape route
    Else
        Factorial = num * Factorial(num – 1)    ' calling itself
    End If
End Function
```

I have used Doubles here because they can cope with very large numbers, and Factorial calculations can produce *very* large results. To test it, attach this code to the **Form_Click**.

```
Private Sub Form_Click ()
    num = InputBox("Enter number", "Factorial")
    newnum = Factorial(CDbl(num))
    Print newnum
End Sub
```

8.5 Multiple forms

Though good programs can be written in a single form, you can sometimes achieve better results more easily by splitting a program over several forms, perhaps linked by a Module. Each form can have a distinctly different layout and set of controls, and can serve a distinct purpose within the program. As we noted when looking at the File and Directory controls, the same form can be incorporated in several different programs if it is applicable.

The relevant commands are:

Insert | Form, or the 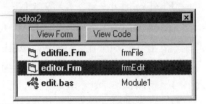 icon, which opens a new, blank form within the project;

Insert | Module, or the icon, which opens a new Basic module;

File | Add File, which pulls an existing file or module into the project;

File | Save File As, which names and saves the *currently active* form or module;

File | Remove File, which removes the *currently active* form or module from the project.

Do take care when saving or removing forms, that the one you want to save or remove is on top, with its title bar highlighted. Get into the habit of doing an initial **Save File As** when you first open a new form, to give it a meaningful name. After that, a regular **Save Project** will ensure that all your forms are safe and up to date.

When you are working with multiple forms, you should keep the Project window open and accessible, so that you can switch easily between them.

An MDI (Multiple Document Interface) form is a special type, allowing your programs to have windows within windows. They are covered in Chapter 14.

8.6 Startup forms

You may have noticed that when you start a program, there is a delay before the form comes into view. This is partly caused by compilation, partly by other checking routines and – if any of the controls use imported graphics or other external data – by opening and loading files. The delay can be so long where there are a number of graphics to import, that your users might start to think that there is a problem. One way to get round this is to have a simple form that loads first – and quickly. It can carry the program title and credits, with an OK button. (Some form of active control is necessary to bring the form to the front of the desktop.) Clicking on the button will hide the startup form and bring the main form into view. There may still be a delay before this is visible, but at least your users will know that things are happening.

To create a start up form, use **Insert | New Form** to bring a new one onto the desktop. Add whatever labels you want, and a button, with code attached to this to transfer the focus to the main form. (An example of this is given in Chapter 11.)

The next job is to specify that the new form is the one to be used at the start. This is done through the **Tools | Options | Project** command. That will open the **Project Options** dialog box.

The key option is **Start Up Form**. Click on this to pull the list down and you will see the names of your forms, plus *Sub Main*. (We will get back to that in a minute.) Select the start up form, click OK, and when you run the program, it will start from there.

8.7 Starting from Sub Main

If all you want on your start up form is a little text and an OK button, you might as well run this through a MsgBox instead. This cannot be run from your main form – that would defeat the object of giving your user something to read while the main form loads. You can, however, run it from a basic module, and execute that on start up.

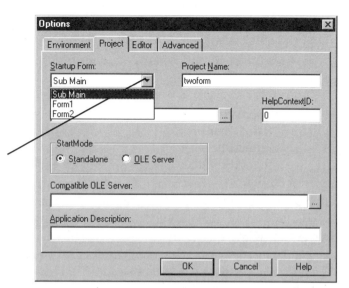

Click on the arrow to drop down the list and select the form or module that you want to run at the start of the program.

Figure 8.3 The Project Options dialog box.

Here's how. Use **Insert | Module**. When the module's code window opens, set up a procedure called *Sub Main* (it **must** be called Main), typing in code along these lines:

```
Sub Main
    MsgBox "Welcome to my World",
    Form1.Show
End Sub
```

You must include the *Show* line to make the main form active. Miss it out, and the program will end as soon as you OK the message box!

To make the program start with Sub Main, set it as the Start Up Form.

8.8 Transferring between forms

There are three aspects to this – transferring the focus of activity, transferring data from one form to another, and picking up the flow of execution as it moves between the forms.

Transferring focus

The simplest way to transfer the focus of activity between forms is with the **SetFocus** method. It is important to note that this can only be used on forms that are open and visible already. To test it out, set up two forms, each containing a command button.

Normally only the first form is visible when the program starts. To make the second visible from the start, write this code in Form1's **Load** procedure:

```
Sub Form1_Load
    Form2.Show
End Sub
```

The code attached to each button should read:

```
Sub Command1_Click ()
    form2.SetFocus     ' or Form1.SetFocus on the second form
End Sub
```

Run the program and you should find that clicking on one button highlights the one on the other form.

Very often you will only want to have one form visible at a time. This is where the **Hide** and **Show** methods come into play. Remove the **Show** line from the **Load** procedure and rewrite the code on the first button to read:

```
Sub Command1_Click ()
    form1.Hide
    form2.Show
    form2.SetFocus
End Sub
```

Do the same to the second button, changing the numbers, and run the program again.

Sometimes you will want to keep two or more forms visible, but only have one active. You see an example of this every time you save or load a file, as Windows will not let you do anything else to an application until you have completed, or cancelled the file dialog box. In these situations, set the Enabled property. Your users only have access to forms where Enabled is True.

```
Form1.Enabled = False
Form2.Enabled = True
```

After this, only Form2 is available to the user.

Data transfer

Data can be transferred between forms through controls, or through global variables. To test this transfer through controls, place a TextBox in each form and add this line to the second form's button:

```
Form1.Text1.Text = Form2.Text1.Text
```

Note the compound nature of the identifier. As long as we are working with controls on the same form, we never have to think about where they are. If you want to refer to a control on a different form, its name must be preceded by the name of the form on which it is placed. As the button that runs this line is on Form2 – and as **.Text** is not really necessary – we could get the same effect with this briefer line:

```
Form1.Text1 = Text1
```

Missing out unnecessary form names may save typing, but including them does make the code more readable.

To transfer data through variables, they must be declared as Global in the general area of a Basic module. Try it. Use **Insert | Module** and in the general window write:

```
Global WhoIsIt
```

Edit the second form's button to include this line at the start:

```
WhoIsIt = InputBox("Who is there?")
```

and this at the end:

```
Form1.Text1 = WhoIsIt
```

Run the program, and you will find that whatever you typed into the InputBox on Form2 appears in the Text box on Form1 when the focus is transferred back to it.

The flow of execution

In earlier versions of Visual Basic, you could move the focus to another form, in the middle of a procedure, and the flow of execution would return to that procedure when the form came back into focus. In Visual Basic 4, that no longer applies. If you have code that must run when the focus returns to a form, it should be written in its **GotFocus** procedure. You will find a fully worked example of this in Chapter 10.

8.9 Procedures and modules

Having created a useful procedure or function, it seems a shame to have it restricted to one program, or to have to rewrite it (or copy it), into every program where you want to use it. There is a solution. If the code is written into a module, which is saved as a separate file, the file can be added into any other program later. Here's how.

- Start with the program containing either the Factorial or the Degree function.
- Use either **Insert| Module** or the 🔧 icon. A new code window, entitled *Module1.bas*, will open. Copy the whole of the procedure across to the module, using the Project window to move between the two.
- With the module window active, use **File | Save File As**, to save the basic module to disk. Call it *fact.bas* or *degree.bas*, as appropriate.
- Close down the project and open a new one, or another existing project.
- Pull in the basic module, with **File | Add File**. Write a short piece of code that will call the function, to check that it is there and working for you.

Any one basic file can be added to as many different programs as you like, but remember that any changes you make to the file will affect every program in which it is used. As one basic module can have any number of procedures and functions within it, you could write all your general purpose functions in the one file, and add this to your programs.

Adding the polygon procedure is not quite as simple, but that is because it uses the Line method. If you look at the formal syntax for this, it starts:

object.Line ...

We didn't bother about specifying the *object*, when we used this earlier in the chapter, as the Line was drawn on the object – the Form – which contained the code. If the code is elsewhere, then the object must be specified, and that creates a problem. If you want the procedure to be general, you cannot know in advance what the target object will be called.

There is a partial solution through the fact that Forms can be used as data types and passed as arguments to a procedure. If we change the first line to read:

Sub polygon (sides, x, y, radius, target As Form)

we now have a variable, *target*, which can be passed to the Line statement:

target.Line (Xstart, Ystart)-(Xnext, Ynext)

In the calling procedure, the target form can be identified by writing its name into the arguments. We can also use the special word **Me**, which refers to the Form in which the code is written. To draw an octagon in the current form we would then use:

polygon 8, 3000, 3000, 1000, Me

8.10 Exercises

1. Write a function to calculate the volume of rectangular objects, from their length, width and height.

2. Write a function that will take in a string of text and output it in reverse. You will need to use the function **Mid(*string, start, number*)**. This slices a *number* of characters from the *string*, from *start* onwards. Test it with various phrases, including '*rats live on no evil star*'.

3. Following on from the last exercise, write a function *Palindrome()* that will test a string of text to see if it reads the same back to front. This function should return an integer value, with -1 indicating True and 0 if the phrase is not palindromic.

4. Build the palindrome function into a program that consists of two forms. The first form should contain a Text Box into which the text should be written. After checking it through the function, the second form should open, displaying a message if a palindrome is found.

Answers to Exercises 1, 2 and 3 are given in Appendix A.

9 Arrays

As well as the normal variable arrays, Visual Basic can handle arrays of controls, and these add a fascinating new dimension to programming.

9.1 Dimensions, elements and subscripts

Arrays provide a compact and efficient means of handling blocks of data. They probably add more to the power of programming than any other feature, for they make it possible to process a mass of data through a standard routine. With an array in use, the same procedure will work just as well with 10 or 10,000 items.

An array is a set of variables – of any type – all with the same name, but with different identifying numbers or *subscripts*. A simple one-dimensioned array can be thought of as a numbered list.

	Names
Names(0)	Fred
Names(1)	Jim
Names(2)	Sally
Names(3)	Dick
Names(4)	Karen
Names(5)	Jo

This array would have been set up with the line:

Dim   Names(5) As String

This has **6** *elements*, numbered 0 to 5. Each can be accessed individually, to read or to change its data, by specifying its subscript: e.g.

Print Names(2)   'displays Sally

Names(4) = Katy   ' replaces *Karen* with *Katy*

A two-dimensional array may be thought of as a table, with numbered rows and columns.

This could be the board for Noughts and Crosses. It would be declared with the line:

Dim OXO(2,2) As String

In the illustration, OXO(0,0) holds "X", and OXO(2,1) holds "O". There is no rule that says you must refer to rows first, then columns. You can think of your array whichever way round you like – as long as you are consistent.

A three-dimensional array, gives you a structure like that of a modern spreadsheet, with multiple pages, each containing a grid of cells. And for those arrays with four or more dimensions, you can think up your own analogies. Visual Basic permits you to have up to 60 dimensions, with subscripts ranging from –32,768 to +32,767. Memory space is a consideration with large arrays. One with three dimensions, each of 100, has 1,000,000 elements. If it is to hold integers, they will require 2 bytes each; longs and singles take 4 bytes; doubles and currency, 8 bytes; and strings 1 byte per character – plus management overheads.

For example:

Dim wages(51,19) As Currency

Will set up an array to hold the weekly wages of 20 workers, and will require a little over 52 * 20 * 8 = 8320 bytes, just over 8Kb.

Dim marks(10,30,25) As Double

This will hold the marks of 5 classes of students, with up to 30 in a class and 25 assignments per student. It will need 10 * 30 * 25 * 8 = 60,000 bytes of storage.

At its simplest, the *Dim* statement gives the size of each dimension, but you can instead specify the first and last subscripts, using the *To* keyword:

Dim dataset(1 To 15, -20 To 20)

This creates a two-dimensional array, with elements running from *dataset(1,-20)* through to *dataset(15,20)*.

If the size of the array will not be known at the start of the program – perhaps because it will be up to the users to specify their storage needs – the dimensions can be omitted from the Dim line. They can then be given later, when they are known, with the **ReDim** statement.

Dim yourdata()   ' in general declarations
ReDim yourdata(rows, cols, pages)   ' in a later procedure

Here *rows*, *cols* and *pages* would be variables holding user-defined values.

An array can be ReDimmed any number of times, but note that existing data is lost unless the **Preserve** option is used. (See the example program in Chapter 14.)

9.2 Arrays and loops

Most data processing in arrays is done through loops, as the routine which works for one element works for all. As the number of elements is known, a **For...Next** structure usually proves to be the logical choice.

Try this simple demonstration. Attach the *input* and the *results* routines to two command buttons, and set up the array in the general declaration window.

Dim dataset(9) As Single

```
Private Sub cmdInput_Click ()
    For element = 0 To 9
        dataset(element) = InputBox("Next value?")
    Next element
End Sub
```

```
Private Sub cmdResults_Click ()
    For element = 0 To 9
        total = total + dataset(element)
    Next element
    average = total / 9
    MsgBox "Total values = " & total & " Average = " & average
End Sub
```

Task 9.1 Place two more command buttons on the form and attach to them routines to display the values in the array, and to edit any chosen element.

9.3 Prime numbers

Finding prime numbers has long been a favourite activity of programmers, because finding bigger numbers faster is a demonstration of the power of a computer and of its program. So why don't we join in the fun too? The following program is based on the fact that a prime number cannot be divided evenly by any other. It starts with 2 as the first prime, and works through the number sequence. As it goes, it divides each number by every prime it knows about, discarding any that leave no remainder. The algorithm takes the shape:

```
If num / primes(n) = Int(num / primes(n)) Then
    primenum = False
```

(The actual program lines are slightly different as the *num* value is held in the Label *lbNum*, so that it can be easily displayed.)

If it reaches the end of the known primes without finding a divisor, then that number is added to the primes set – and the primes are, of course, held in an array.

lblNum is used to hold and to display the number currently being checked by the search routine.
lblFound is updated as each new prime is identified.
Without the scroll bar, the Text box could only display the first 300 or so primes.

PrimeBox

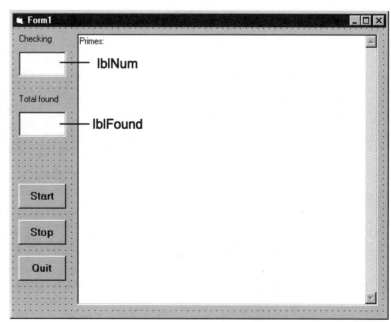

Figure 9.1 The form layout for the primes program.

95

The program has two limitations, which will prevent you from using it to get into the Guinness Book of Records. The first is the size of the array. In the demo program this is set at 1000. You can push this as high as your computer can manage. The second limitation is time. The first couple of hundred primes are found in a matter of seconds, but the further you go, the longer it takes to check each number against the ever-growing primes set.

The form layout for this program is shown in Figure 9.1. You will notice that I have included a Stop button in the design, so that you can halt the search when you grow bored. The button sets the variable *finished* to True. This causes the search loop to end, and the results to be displayed.

You will also see that there is a Scroll bar on the Text box used to display the results. To get this, set the Text box's *Scroll bars* property to *2 - Vertical*.

```
general declarations
    Dim primes(1000) As Integer             ' or as many as you like
    Dim finished As Integer
    Dim primelist As String

Private Sub cmdStart_Click ()
    Dim n As Integer
    finished = False
    primelist = "Primes:"                    ' header text for the display
    lblNum = 2                               ' start of number sequence
    lblFound = 0
    primes(n) = 2                            ' the first known prime
    Do                                       ' search routine loop
        lblNum = lblNum + 1
        primenum = True
        For n = 0 To lblFound                ' divide by known primes
            If lblNum / primes(n) = Int(lblNum / primes(n)) Then
                primenum = False
                Exit For                     ' quit when a divisor is found
            End If
        Next n
        If primenum Then                     ' if no divisor found
            lblFound = lblFound + 1
            primes(lblFound) = lblNum        ' add to primes set
            primelist = primelist & " " & lblNum   ' add to display string
        End If
        DoEvents                             ' allow check for Stop Button
    Loop Until finished Or lblFound = 1000
    PrimeBox = primelist                     ' copy result to TextBox
End Sub
```

This comes up when Loop is finished ⟶ (handwritten annotation pointing to PrimeBox = primelist line)

The **DoEvents** statement near the end of the loop returns control, briefly, to the operating system, so that it can check for any button clicks or other events. Without it, there would be no way of halting the routine, except through **[Ctrl]+[Break]**. Its presence allows the **Stop** procedure to be activated.

```
Private Sub cmdStop_Click ()
    finished = True
End Sub
```

Note that the whole purpose of this is to force an exit from the search loop – the flow of execution remains within the **Start_Click** procedure, but moves on to display the results.

9.4 Control arrays

The control array is one of the great delights of Visual Basic, and not one that you will have come across in Pascal or traditional Basics. In the same way that variables can be grouped and handled *en masse* through variable arrays, so controls can be grouped into control arrays. All types of control are suitable for this treatment, though Forms, Command Button, Images and Picture boxes, Labels and Text boxes are probably the most useful ones to group. An array of Forms is almost essential in MDI structures (See Chapter 14); an array of Buttons can simplify the code needed to get instructions from the user; an array of Images is a great aid to animation (see Chapter 12); an array of Labels or Text Boxes can hold data – like a variable array – and display it at the same time. It is this latter feature that we will exploit in the next example.

Stacks of controls

A stack is an area of memory accessed on a Last In, First Out basis. In the jargon, data is *pushed* onto a stack and *popped* off it. The operating system and other programs written at machine level use the *Stack* (a predefined part of memory) to track the flow of execution to and from sub-routines, and for temporary storage of data. We will use a simulated stack to hold values in a program that performs calculations using Reverse Polish notation. The first hand-held calculators used this as it is the most efficient way of doing arithmetic – at least, from the program's point of view.

In Reverse Polish, operators follow the values on which they are to work, e.g.

> **2 2 +**

is the same as 2 + 2 in normal notation. With a compound calculation, you start from the leftmost operator, use that on the two previous values, the result providing one of the values for the next operator. For example, the sum (5 + 4 - 3) * 2 in normal arithmetic becomes this:

> **2 3 4 5 + - *   first operation   5 4 + = 9**
> **2 3 9 - *   second operation 9 3 - = 6**
> **2 6 *   third operation   6 2 * = 12**

Implementing it in a program is easy, because there are only two basic rules for the computer to follow as it takes in the string of values and operators:

1 If you meet a number, push it on the stack

2 If you meet an operator, pop the last two numbers off the stack, use the operator on them and push the result back on the stack.

If you were writing the program in assembler, you could use the real stack. As we are working in a high-level language, we will need an array to act as a stack. If we use an array of Labels, we will be able to see what's going on.

9.5 Creating a control array

A control array can be created at design time, or merely started then, with extra elements added at runtime from within the code. We will use that technique in some later programs. The elements can be placed directly on the form, or within a frame. As a frame makes it easier to adjust the display, we will use one here.

- Create a frame, then draw a Label within the frame.

- Name the Label *lblStack*, erase its caption and set its border to 1-Solid. If you want to set other properties of the Label, do so now. The simplest way to create an array of identical objects is by copying – so get the first one looking right!

- Move the Frame to the very top left of the Form. This is important, for reasons which will become clear in a moment.

- Select the Label, and give the **Edit | Copy** command.

- Next, click on the Frame to select it – this is important.

- Now do **Edit | Paste** and you will see this message box on the screen:

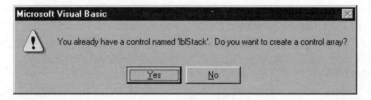

- When you answer 'Yes', a copy of the Label will appear at the top left corner of the Frame. If you had not selected the Frame first, the Label would have been placed directly on the Form, and no amount of shuffling would have got it into the Frame!

- Check the Properties window and you will see that the new control is named *lblStack(1)*, and the old one has been renamed *lblStack(0)*.

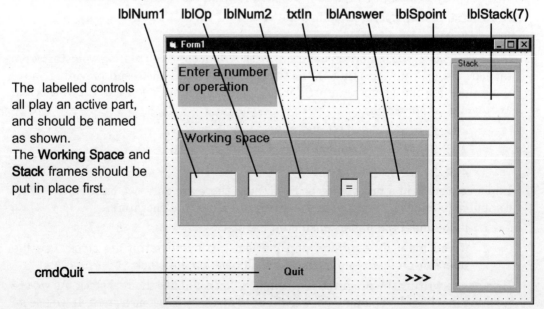

The labelled controls all play an active part, and should be named as shown.
The **Working Space** and **Stack** frames should be put in place first.

Figure 9.2 The Reverse Polish form in use.

Create another 6 or so *lblStack* labels in the same way, and arrange them one above the other in the Frame. Your control array is ready. The enclosing Frame can now be moved to its final position and the rest of the controls added to give a layout similar to that shown. *lblNum1, lblNum2, lblOp* and *lblAnswer* are all Labels used to hold and display data during calculations; *txtIn* is a TextBox for collecting inputs from the user; *lblSpoint* is a Label that is moved up and down beside the *lblStack* array to indicate the current top of the stack. It is purely decorative and can be omitted.

Code design

The code breaks conveniently into two blocks – one attached to *txtIn* to collect the inputs, and a free-standing procedure to handle the calculations. The *txtIn* code will run off the *KeyPress* event, when [Enter] is pressed. Its design follows the rules set out earlier, with a little extra to prevent stack overflow and to move the pointer.

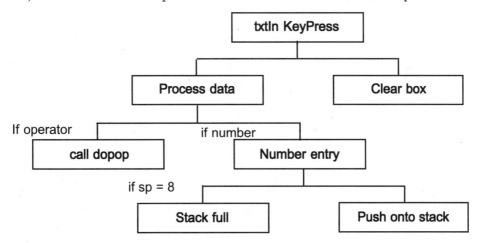

The stack pointer, that tracks the progress through the *lblStack* array, has to be accessed by this and the calculating procedure. It is held in the general variable *sp*.

The code is a simple translation of the design. You will almost certainly have to adjust the value in the line that moves *lblSpoint*, as this depends entirely on the size of the *lblStack* controls. Mine were 500 Twips high.

```
Private Sub txtIn_KeyPress (keyascii As Integer)      General Declaration
    If keyascii = 13 Then                             Dim sp As Integer
        If txtIn = "+" Or txtIn = "-" Or txtIn= "*" Or txtIn= "/" Then dopop
        If IsNumeric(txtIn) Then
            If sp = 8 Then                            ' if there are 8 in the array
                MsgBox "Stack Overflow", 48
            Else
                lblStack(sp) = txtIn                  ' push number onto stack
                sp = sp + 1                           ' move the stack pointer
                lblSpoint.Top = lblSpoint.Top - 500   ' and the arrow display
            End If
        End If
        txtIn= ""                                     ' clear the input area
    End If
End Sub
```

The pop-and-calculate design can be simplified to this:

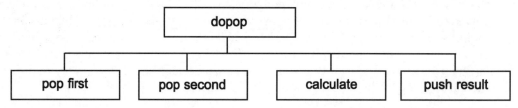

The implementation is a little more complex. We should check that we haven't reached the bottom of the stack before attempting to pop; and the different 'calculate' operations must be handled by a set of *Ifs* or a *Case* structure. The whole routine could have been included in the **KeyPress** code, but splitting it off into a separate procedure makes the program more readable.

```
Sub dopop ()
    If sp = 0 Then                          ' error-trap – can be omitted at first
        MsgBox "Bottom of stack", 48
        Exit Sub
    End If

    sp = sp - 1                             ' move the stack pointer
    lblSpoint.Top = lblSpoint.Top + 500     ' and the arrow display
    lblNum1 = lblStack(sp)                  ' pop the first number
    lblStack(sp) = ""                       ' clear the stack display

    If sp = 0 Then                          ' more error trapping
        MsgBox "Bottom of stack", 48
        Exit Sub
    End If

    sp = sp - 1                             ' move the stack pointer
    lblNum2 = lblStack(sp)                  ' pop the next number
    lblOp = txtIn                           ' display symbol
    Select Case lblOp                       ' calculate
    Case "+"
        lblAnswer = Val(lblNum1) + lblNum2  ' force numeric +
    Case "-"
        lblAnswer = lblNum1 - lblNum2
    Case "*"
        lblAnswer = lblNum1 * lblNum2
    Case "/"
        lblAnswer = lblNum1 / lblNum2
    End Select

    lblStack(sp) = lblAnswer                ' push the result onto the stack
    sp = sp + 1                             ' move the pointer again
End Sub
```

9.6 Indexing and event handling

In the last example, the control array was used for displaying and holding values, but they can also be used actively. Look at the code window for the Click or any other event of an arrayed control and you will see that the definition line includes the argument:

...(..Index As Integer..)

The *index* of a control array is the same as the subscript for a variable array, and serves to identify which of the controls has been activated. In practice, this allows one block of code to serve for all the controls in the array, which is just what you need if they are all there to do identical, or very similar jobs.

As a demonstration of using the index and of event handling, here is a simple on-screen calculator. It uses two control arrays – one for the digit 'buttons' and one for the symbols.

Labels are used for both arrays.

The **lblDigit** array numbering matches the display, with **lblDigit(10)** being the decimal point.

In the **lblOperator** array: 0 is =; 1 is +; 2 is -; 3 is *; 4 is /.

The Command Buttons are individual controls, as each performs a distinct job.

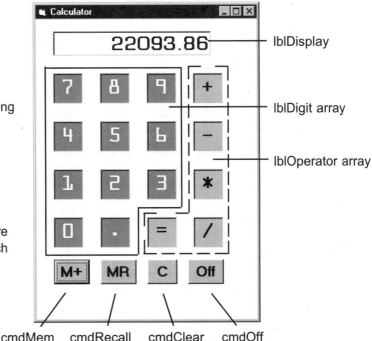

Figure 9.3 The Calculator Form, showing the controls.

Form design

The basic layout is shown above. In this case the control arrays have been placed directly on the Form. I have used Labels, rather than Buttons for the digits and operators so that their background colours can be changed. Remember to set up the Font, Border and Color properties of the first control of each array, before copying to create the rest.

Code design

There are two major blocks of code here, on the Click procedures of the *digit* and the *operator* control arrays. We will tackle them first, then turn to the smaller blocks.

A Click on a *digit* can mean either start a new number, or add another figure to the number that is building in the display. We can handle this by having a variable, *newnumber*, which is set to True when an *operator* is selected, after which the user will be starting a new number. *newnumber* must be declared at the general level.

Building the number in the display is done by the line:

```
lblDisplay = lblDisplay & lblDigit(index)
```

This takes the Caption from the clicked digit and joins it to the display string.

```
Private Sub lblDigit_Click (index As Integer)
    If newnumber Then                    'erase old display first
        lblDisplay = ""
        newnumber = False
    End If
    lblDisplay = lblDisplay & lblDigit(index)
End Sub
```

Handling the operators is a little more complex, and we must stop for a moment and think about how a real pocket calculator is used. When an operator is selected, it is not acted upon immediately, but is put on hold until after the next number has been entered and the next operator selected. Take the sequence: *12 + 34 =* When the calculator meets '+' it will store the 12 and make a note that there is an add to do. Only when it reaches '=' will it do the sum.

Where there is a sequence of operations, each will only be performed when the next is entered – or possibly not even then, if the current operation has higher priority than the previous one. Multiplication and division should be performed before addition and subtraction; powers, roots and other functions have higher priority than arithmetic operators. (Contrast this with the simplicity of Reverse Polish calculation.) We will ignore the problem of priority, so that we can focus on using control arrays.

The simplified code for the operator symbols take the form:

1 If there is no operator in store
      store the number in the display
   Else
      get the second number from the display
      do the appropriate calculation
      discard the stored operator

2 If the selected operator is not =
      store it for next time

3 set the newnumber variable to true

This translates to the code:

```
Private Sub lblOperator_Click (index As Integer)
    If op = "" Then                      ' first number coming
        n1 = lblDisplay
    Else                                 ' deal with last operation
        n2 = lblDisplay                  ' get second number
        Select Case op                   ' calculate
            Case "+"
                lblDisplay = n1 + n2
```

```
            Case "-"
                lblDisplay = n1 - n2
            Case "*"
                lblDisplay = n1 * n2
            Case "/"
                lblDisplay = n1 / n2
        End Select
        op = ""
    End If
    If index > 0 Then              ' not the = button
        op = lblOperator(index)    ' store next operation
    End If
    newnumber = True
End Sub
```

The number values and the operator are only actively used inside this procedure, but must be accessible to *cmdClear*, so that they can be reset. Their variables must be declared at the general level. Others needed here are *newnumber*, which we met earlier, and *memory*, which we will get to shortly.

```
general declarations
    Dim n1 As Currency, n2 As Currency
    Dim op As String
    Dim newnumber
    Dim memory As Currency
```

All that is needed at Load time is to set the *newnumber* variable.

```
Private Sub Form_Load ()
    newnumber = False
End Sub
```

The Command Button procedures each contain a single line to do a simple job.

```
Private Sub cmdClearn_Click ()
    lblDisplay = ""               ' wipe the display
End Sub


Private Sub cmdMem_Click ()
    memory = lblDisplay           ' copy the display to the memory variable
End Sub


Private Sub cmdRecall_Click ()
    lblDisplay = memory           ' and copy it back when wanted
End Sub


Private Sub cmdOff_Click ()
    End                           ' quit the program.
End Sub
```

103

9.7 Exercises

1. Add code to the average program example given in Section 9.2, so that it will:
    (1) display the contents of the array;

    (2) allow the user to change the value held in any element;

    (3) work out the maximum and minimum values in the set;

    (4) sort the set into order.

2. Design and write a program that will allow the user to enter text into a Text box, then change its colour by selecting a coloured Label from an array. If the array was named *lblPalette*, the key line would read:

    Text1.ForeColor = lblPalette(Index).BackColor

3. Design and write a program to create a Noughts and Crosses board. The board should be made from an array of 9 Text boxes. Players will enter their move by clicking on a square and typing X or O. The program should check for completed lines, and for a full board and announce the winner or a draw.

4. Add a procedure to the Noughts and Crosses game so that the computer can play a sensible game.

    Possible solutions to Exercise 1, 2 and 3 are given in Appendix A; a solution for Exercise 4 is included in the Lecturer's Supplement disk.

    The files for the *Reverse Polish* and *Calculator* programs are available from the Visual Basic page at the author's Web site: http://www.tcp.co.uk/~macbride

10 Interacting with the system

Almost everything involves some interaction with the system. The focus here is on four particular aspects – the computer's clock, Timers, the Windows Clipboard and access to files.

10.1 Date and Time

Visual Basic has a comprehensive set of functions for accessing the system clock and for handling dates and time. They are efficient and simple to use – though not without their peculiarities.

There are five functions that can read the system clock and return values to a program:

Function	Returns	Example
Now	date and time	29/03/94 15:14:35
Date	date as numbers	29/03/04
Date$	date as formatted string	03-29-1994
Time/Time$	time in 24 hour clock	15:14:35

Test them by displaying the values in a message box.

MsgBox "Today is " & Date

You may find that the *Now* and *Date* dates are displayed in a different format, as this depends upon the settings in the International section of the Windows Control Panel. Whatever those settings, Date$ always uses the US format "Month-Date-Year".

Visual Basic's string-handling facilities can recognise a number of date formats. Whether you present it with "29/3/94", "29-03-94", "29 Mar 1994", "29th March 1994" or any similar combination, it will treat it as the same date. Dates are held internally as numeric date values, where 1 was 31st December 1899; as I write, the day is number 34,422. (Historians and futurists may be interested to know that the system can handle dates back to 100 AD and forward to the end of the 10th millenium.) The fractional part of the date value is the time.

Date/Time values have two practical implications: we can calculate with them, and we can use the Format function to force them into a different display style.

Calculating with dates

Counting the days until the end of term? Try this:

```
Private Sub Form_Click ()
    MsgBox "Today is " & Date$
    holiday = InputBox("When is the next holiday?")
    holidateval = CVDate(holiday)                    'see below
    howlong = holidateval - Date
    MsgBox "You have" & howlong & " days to wait"
End Sub
```

CVDate() will convert any valid date string to a number value.

Task 10.1 Type the Holiday calculator into the Form_Click procedure and test it out with a variety of dates in different formats. How comprehensive is Visual Basic's date recognition?

Date and time formats

The **Format**() function can be used with any kind of number value, though its interest to us at the moment is purely display styles for dates and time. The syntax is:

Format(value, "format string")

The format string recognises certain characters as special. Key ones are:

d	Day of the month number, with no leading zero
dd	Day of the month number with leading zero
ddd	Day of the week, abbreviated
dddd	Day of the week in full
m/mm	Month number, without/with leading zero
mmm	Month name, abreviated
mmmm	Month name in full
yy	Year as two digit
yyyy	Year in full
h/hh	Hours
m/mm	Minutes, when used with h
s/ss	Seconds
AM/PM	Use 12-hour clock with added AM or PM

Examples

"ddd d mmm yyyy"	Tues 29th Mar 1994
"dd-mm-yy"	29-03-94
"hh:mm AM/PM"	03:45 PM

10.2 The Timer

From time to Timers – why not? Any code attached to a Timer control is executed regularly, at a predetermined interval, no matter what else is happening elsewhere in the program. The interval can be set at the Properties window or in the code, and is given in 1/1000th of a second.

Task 10.2 Place a Timer ( ) on a form, along with a Label named *lblClock*. Add the code given below to the relevant events.

```
Private Sub Form_Load()
    Form1.Show              ' ensure that the form is visible
    Timer1.Interval = 1000  ' once a second
    Timer1.Enabled = True   ' Turn it on
End Sub
```

```
Private Sub Timer1_Timer()
    lblClock = Format(Time, "hh:mm:ss AM/PM")        ' Format is not necessary
    Beep                                             ' here for demo purposes
End Sub
```

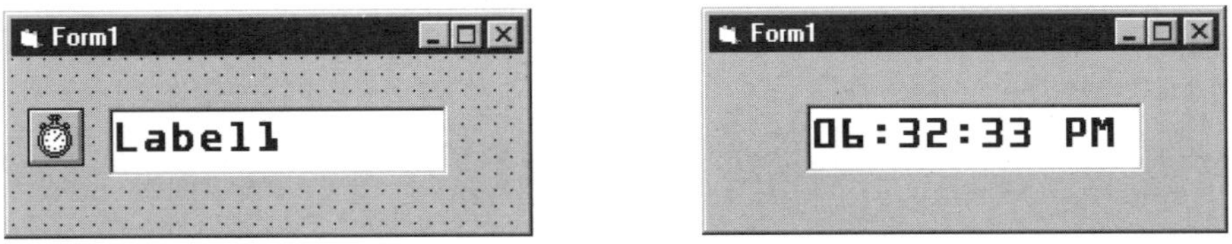

Figure 10.1 Timers become invisible when the program is run.

Add the same controls and code to any program and you can have a clock ticking away in the background. (You do not really want that *Beep*!)

The maximum interval you can set for a Timer is 65,535 – just over a minute. If this is not long enough, then here is a way round the problem. If you set up a general variable, or one declared as *Static* within the Timer procedure, its value will be retained from one execution to the next, and it can be used as a counter. To see how this works, place a Timer on a form, setting its interval to 1000, i.e. one second.

```
general declaration
    Dim SecondsCount
Private Sub Form_Load ()
    limit = InputBox("How many minutes?", "EggTimer")
    SecondsCount = limit * 60                        ' convert to seconds
    Timer1.Enabled = True                            ' turn the timer on
End Sub
Private Sub Timer1_Timer ()
    Static seconds
    seconds = seconds + 1
    If seconds = SecondsCount Then
        MsgBox "Your egg is ready"
        Timer1.Enabled = False                       ' turn it off
    End If
End Sub
```

Use Timers to create fixed delays, to limit the time the system waits for an input from the user, or for animation. (See Chapter 13.)

10.3 Using the Clipboard

If you – and your users – are happy working with the keyboard shortcuts ([Ctrl]+[X] to Cut, [Ctrl]+[C] to Copy, and [Ctrl]+[V] to Paste), then you can use the standard Windows Clipboard for cutting and pasting text without having to write a single line of code. The shortcuts are there, simply because you are in Windows.

If you want to do the job properly and give you users Cut and Paste buttons or menu options, you can access the Clipboard directly, and use its methods and functions in your programs. Graphics, as well as text, can be copied to and from the Clipboard – we'll stick to text for this demonstration.

There are two crucial routines that work with the Clipboard:

- the **SetText** method will copy a selected block of text into the Clipboard;
- the **GetText** function will copy it into a control within the program.

The text is selected in the usual way – by highlighting with the mouse – and recognised by the system as **SelText**. With all the heavy work done by Visual Basic, the actual code is very short.

To see how it works, set up a form containing a Text box, *Text1*, and three Command Buttons, named *cmdCut*, *cmdCopy* and *cmdPaste*.

With only four controls to place and four lines of code to write, it shouldn't take you long to implement this program. Name the Buttons *cmdCut*, *cmdCopy* and *cmdPaste*.

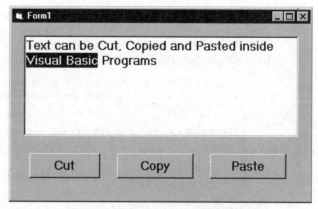

Figure 10.2 A simple form to test the Clipboard facilities.

The **Copy** operation is the simplest.

```
Private Sub cmdCopy_Click ()
    Clipboard.SetText   Text1.SelText
End Sub
```

Note that there is just a space, not an = sign, betwen **SetText** and the incoming text.

The **Cut** operation is the same, with the addition of one line to erase the selected text.

```
Private Sub cmdCut_Click ()
    Clipboard.SetText   Text1.SelText
    Text1.SelText = ""
End Sub
```

With **Paste**, we have to remember how the normal Paste facility works – it overwrites selected text, or inserts at the current cursor position. This is also held in **SelText**.

```
Private Sub cmdPaste_Click ()
    Text1.SelText = Clipboard.GetText()
End Sub
```

This line would work, but it would replace the *whole* of the text in the Text box by whatever was in the Clipboard, rather than adding text at a selected point.

```
Text1 = Clipboard.GetText()
```

Task 10.3 Implement the Clipboard program outlined above. To prove to yourself that this really is accessing the standard Clipboard, run the program and cut and paste between its Text box and another program that handles text.

10.4 Worked example – text editor

This next program takes the use of the Clipboard further to add extra interaction with the system, and also introduces List boxes, which we will return to shortly when we look at File and Directory controls. It creates a simple menu-driven text editor, with Cut-and-Paste, Font control and printing facilities. The extra interaction with the system lies in reading the system's font list and sending text to the printer.

The **Text1** Text Box fills the entire form.

The **cboFont** Combo box and the **fraSize** Frame are only visible when the Font Name and Font Size routines are selected.

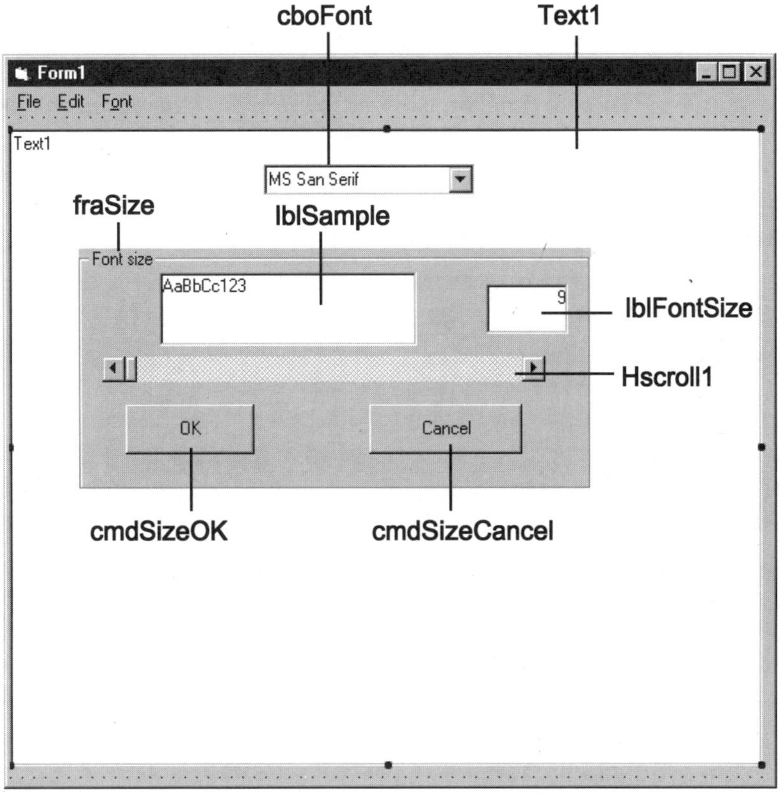

Figure 10.3 The Editor form, showing active controls.

Anyone who has ever tried to write a text editor in a traditional programming language will know that it takes a lot of complex code to manage the editing. Every keystoke must be scanned and checked separately, and intricate string-handling is needed to cope with deletions, insertions, word-wrap and similar activities. In Visual Basic, all we have to do is slap a Text Box on the form and leave the system to look after the text. The only code we need is for the higher-level actions of printing, formatting and Cut-and-Paste. There are two areas that we must look at more closely before attempting to put it all together.

Using Combo boxes

The Combo box is a combination of a small Text Box into which values can be typed, and a list from which they can be selected. Its initial value, i.e. what shows in the slot, is held by its Text property, and can be set at design time or run time. Here it is done in the **Form_Load** procedure by the line:

```
cboFont.Text = "Arial"
```

The rest of the list must be added by the *AddItem* method at runtime. Here, the items are drawn from the list of names held by the **Screen** object in its F*onts()* array. The object also stores, in *FontCount*, the number of names. This leads us to the routine:

```
For n = 0 To Screen.FontCount - 1
    cboFont.AddItem  Screen.Fonts(n)
Next n
```

The *AddItem* method stores the items in the box's *List()* property which acts like any array. Items are added at the end of the list, or placed in alphabetical order if the control's *Sorted* property is set to True. To pick up the selected item when the box is used in the program, we can use *ListIndex*. This value will be changed by the Click event and should be collected during its procedure.

```
Text1.FontName = cboFont.List(cboFont.ListIndex)
```

Menu and program structure

As everything is run off the menu system, this gives us the program's structure.

File	Edit	Font
Print	Cut	Bold
Exit	Copy	Italic
Yes	Paste	Name
No		Size

Print

The Print procedure copies the text from the Text box to the Printer object. If the font settings are also to be used on the printer, then they must be copied over first. In Windows, all printing is handled through Print Manager, and nothing is transferred to the printer itself until the whole document has been sent out by the program. In practice, this means we must close off the printing with the **EndDoc** method.

```
Sub mnuPrint_Click ()
    printer.FontName = Text1.FontName
    printer.FontBold = Text1.FontBold
    printer.FontItalic = Text1.FontItalic
    printer.FontSize = Text1.FontSize
    printer.Print Text1
    printer.EndDoc
End Sub
```

Exit

This can be identical to the one in the menu example in Chapter 5, or could use indexed items, as shown on page 113.

Edit

In any program's Edit menu, choices are sometimes 'greyed' to show that they are unavailable. You cannot Cut or Copy if nothing has been selected; you cannot Paste if the Clipboard is empty. The enabling/disabling can best be handled by the Click procedure of headers, so that when the user opens a menu, options are turned on or off before it is displayed. Here, the code goes in the **mnuEdit** item's **Click** procedure.

```
Private Sub mnuEdit_Click ()
    If Clipboard.GetText() = "" Then
        mnuPaste.Enabled = False
    Else
        mnuPaste.Enabled = True
    End If
    If Text1.SelText = "" Then
        mnuCopy.Enabled = False
        mnuCut.Enabled = False
    Else
        mnuCopy.Enabled = True
        mnuCut.Enabled = True
    End If
End Sub
```

Cut, **Copy** and **Paste** are identical to those used earlier, but attached to menu options.

Fonts

The **Bold** and **Italic** options are best run as toggle switches, for these properties can only be either True of False. The **Not** operator handles toggles beautifully:

```
Text1.FontBold = Not Text1.FontBold
```

If *FontBold* was True on entry to this line, it will be False on exit, and vice versa. A second line is needed to toggle the *Checked* property of the menu, so that the tick appears when FontBold is set to True. Both properties could be set at design time, but as they are on separate controls – so that there is an increased likelihood of forgetting to set one or the other – it is safest to set them together in the **Form_Load** procedure. Look out for the relevant lines. Here are the **Click** procedures for **Bold** and **Italic**.

```
Private Sub mnuBold_Click ()
    Text1.FontBold = Not Text1.FontBold
    mnuBold.Checked = Not mnuBold.Checked
End Sub
Private Sub mnuItalic_Click ()
    Text1.FontItalic = Not Text1.FontItalic
    mnuItalic.Checked = Not mnuItalic.Checked
End Sub
```

The *mnuName* menu option simply makes the *cboFont* ComboBox visible.

```
Private Sub mnuName_Click ()
    cboFont.Visible = True
End Sub
```

Making a selection from a ComboBox list triggers its Click procedure. We can then pick up the selection from the Click and transfer it to Text1 (and also to the Sample label in the Font Size frame), then hide the list again.

```
Private Sub cboFont_Click ()
    Text1.FontName = cboFont.List(cboFont.ListIndex)
    lblSample.FontName = cboFont.List(cboFont.ListIndex)
    cboFont.Visible = False
End Sub
```

The **Size** routine could also have used a Combobox, as most people only want a limited selection of FontSizes – 9, 12, 18 and 30 would cover most requirements – and a Combobox does have a type-in facility for those who want to be different. However, a ScrollBar is easy to implement and gives your users free choice. As a bare ScrollBar would be a little confusing, the one in this program is installed in a Frame, accompanied by a label to display the current size, and OK and Cancel buttons.

The menu procedure merely makes the *fraSize* Frame visible. Within the frame, a Change event on the scroll bar updates the number in *lblFontSize* display and the FontSize of *lblFontSize* and *lblSample*, but not the FontSize property of the Text Box. The value is not transferred to there until *cmdSizeOK* is clicked. Both this and *cmdSizeCancel* hide the frame.

```
Private Sub mnuSize_Click ()
    fraSize.Visible = True
End Sub

Private Sub HScroll1_Change ()
    lblFontSize = HScroll1
    lblFontSize.FontSize = HScroll1
    lblSample.FontSize = HScroll1
End Sub

Private Sub cmdSizeOK_Click ()
    Text1.FontSize = Hscroll1              'copy value to Text1
    fraSize.Visible = False            ' hide the Frame
End Sub

Private Sub cmdSizeCancel_Click ()
    fraSize.Visible = False               ' hide the Frame
End Sub
```

Initialisation

The text properties, some of the menu item properties, the Clipboard and the FontList must all be initialised at the start of the program, on the **Form_Load** procedure.

```
Private Sub Form_Load ()
    Text1.FontBold = False          ' turn Bold off
    mnuBold.Checked = False         ' and its menu checkmark
    Text1.FontItalic = False        ' turn Italic off
    mnuItalic.Checked = False       ' and its checkmark
    Text1.FontSize = 9              ' set the size of the text
    HScroll1 = 9                    ' and the scroll bar's default value
    Clipboard.Clear                 ' remove any data from the Clipboard
    cboFont.Visible = False         ' hide the cboFont Combo box
    Text1.FontName = "Arial"
    cboFont.Text = "Arial"          ' set up the cboFont values
    For n = 0 To Screen.FontCount - 1
        cboFont.AddItem Screen.Fonts(n)
    Next n
End Sub
```

10.5 Indexes in menus

Instead of giving each menu item a unique name, you can group related ones into indexed sets. This approach works well where the code is similar or interlinked, as you have only one block of code to write for all the related items.

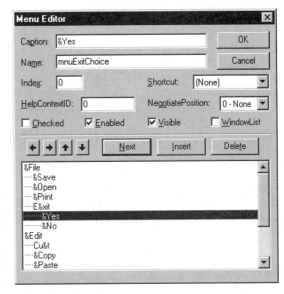

To create a set of indexed menu items, define the first as normal, and type 0 in the **Index** slot. Define the other items, giving the same name to each but with the **Index** numbers rising through 1, 2, 3, etc. When you close the Menu Editor and open the code window for any of those items, it will take you to the same procedure, with an '**Index As Integer**' parameter.

For example, the *Exit* sub-menu has '*Yes*' and '*No*' options – to give your users chance to confirm that they want to quit, though only the '*Yes*' actually needs code. We could handle these through indexed items, named as **mnuExitChoice**. Its code would take the form:

```
Private Sub mnuExitChoice_Click(Index As Integer)
    If Index = 0 Then End
End Sub
```

Here's another example of indexed menu items, and this makes fuller use of the index. The menu offers a choice of colours for the text – it can be slotted into the existing system as an extra item of the Font menu.

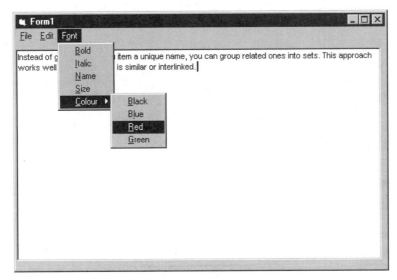

Figure 10.4 The colour sub-menu can be fitted into the Font menu.

In the code, we have an array *colour()* holding the appropriate values, in the same order as on the menu. All we need to do is use the Index of the menu as the subscript of the array.

```
Private Sub mnuColChoice_Click(Index As Integer)
    Dim colour(3) As Long
    colour(0) = 0                    ' black
    colour(1) = &HFF0000             ' blue
    colour(2) = &HFF&                ' red
    colour(3) = &HFF00&              ' green

    Text1.ForeColor = colour(Index)
End Sub
```

If you want to know what values to use to define a colour, set that colour in the Properties box for any object, and read the values off the display.

Task 10.4 Implement the Text Editor program, setting the inital properties to your own preferences. Add options to the Font menu to Underline text, and to restore text to normal.

10.6 File and directory controls

Visual Basic has three controls designed to make file management simple. They are all varieties of ListBoxes with built-in vertical scroll bars that come into play when the list to be displayed is too long for the box.

A **Drive List box** displays, and allows you to select from, the drives on the system. The property *.Drive* holds the current drive.

A **Dir List box** displays and allows you to select from the directories on the current drive. Its *.Drive* property can be linked to a DriveListBox, and *Path* stores the current drive and directory path.

A **File List box** displays, and allows you to select from, the files in the current directory. This also has *Drive* and *Path* properties, plus *FileName*, which holds the name of a selected file, and *Pattern*, which holds the file specification. The default for this is *.*, i.e. every file in the directory.

These are the same controls that you will find in the Save Open or Print File dialog boxes of any Windows 3.1 application. They are normally used together, in conjunction with a dual-purpose Text Box or two separate Text Boxes for the file specification pattern and the selected filename. Changes in the **Drive** are fed to the **Dir List** and to the **File List**; changes in the **Dir List** and the file specification are passed to the **File List**; the selected filename is passed to the filename TextBox.

Note: One of Visual Basic's optional controls is the Common Dialog Box. This also gives access to files, combining the above controls with routines for saving, opening and printing. We will look at the Common Dialog Box in Chapter 15.

10.7 Worked example – File Selector

The following program uses the three List boxes to select a file, but having selected one, you really ought to do something with it. I have chosen to write a rename routine attached to a Command Button. You may prefer to do something else – or nothing at all – with your selected file. In the next section, the File Selector form is incorporated into another program, to give it file-handling facilities. We shall turn to other aspects of file management in the next few chapters.

When you place the List boxes on the form, bear in mind that the Drive box is a drop-down List, and should therefore only be deep enough to display one line at a time, but when it drops down, it might overlap whatever is beneath. The Font, Color and other properties can be set as usual, but they are probably best left at their standard settings – the more your file selection display matches the ones in other Windows 3.1 applications, the better.

The **Drive**, **Dir** and **File List** boxes arranged on a Form, with two **Text Boxes**, *txtFilename* and *txtFileSpec*, and two Command Buttons. While you can use any layout you like, one which follows the Windows standard layout will make your users feel at home.

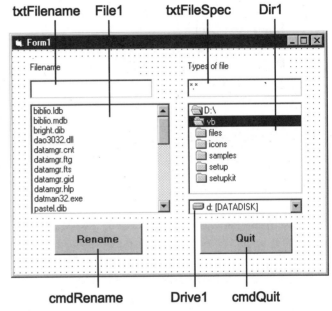

Figure 10.5 The Drive, Dir and File List boxes give simple access to files.

Linking the Directory data

The only routines that are needed here are to pass values from one control to another as they are changed – and most are attached to the **Change** event. Note that the key value from the **Drive** List box is the *Drive*, but this is passed to the *Path* of the **Dir** and **File List** boxes.

```
Sub Drive1_Change ()
    Dir1.Path = Drive1.Drive
    File1.Path = Drive1.Drive
End Sub

Sub Dir1_Change ()
    File1.Path = Dir1.path
End Sub
```

```
Sub FileSpec_Change ()
    File1.Pattern = Filespec
End Sub
```

The program uses an open-ended file specification box – the users can type in anything they like. In some programs, you would want to restrict the selection to files with certain extensions, and for this you should use a List box or Combo, into which you have written the acceptable file patterns. If you were looking for graphic files, for example, you might only want to display those with a *.PCX or *.BMP pattern.

Notice that the code has been attached to the **Change** event. As a result, the file list display is updated with every keystroke. If you prefer, you could use the **KeyPress** event, and only copy the Pattern across after [Enter] is pressed. There is no Windows standard here, you will see both techniques in use.

With the **File List** box, the important event is the **Click**, which responds to the user selecting a file.

```
Sub File1_Click ()
    txtFilename = File1.FileName
End Sub
```

What you get out of these List boxes are the names of a selected Drive, Directory and File. The current drive/directory is *not* changed, any more than selecting a file opens it. If you want them changed, you must do so explicitly with:

```
ChDrive drive1          ' in Drive1_Change
CdDir  Dir1.Path        ' in Dir1_Change
```

Paths and filenames

Sometimes you will want to keep the program in one base directory, while drawing in files from elsewhere. In this case, the Path value must be added to the start of the filename before you attempt to access it. When doing this, we have to watch out for a little peculiarity of the Windows system.

- A path to the root will look like "C:\", with a backslash after the drive letter;
- a path to a directory, e.g."C:\VB\FILES", will have no backslash after it.

When we add a filename to the end of a *directory* path, we must insert a backslash between the path and the name. That gives us this code for creating full path-filenames:

```
If Right(dir1.Path, 1) = "\" Then
    fname = Dir1.Path & txtFilename
Else
    fname = Dir1.Path & "\" & txtFilename
End If
```

The **Right(*string,number*)** function slices the given *number* of characters off the right end of the *string*. In this case, we are using it to check the last, single, character of the path.

Renaming files

So what are you going to do with your file, now that it has been selected and the filename organised? Here is a rename routine, which you may find useful for tidying up your directories. If a file has been selected, it first creates a full path-filename combination for that, then collects a new name through an InputBox – and creates its path-filename. Finally, it renames the file using the **Name** statement. The confirm routine at the end could be omitted if preferred.

```
Sub cmdRename_Click ()
    If txtFilename <> "" Then
        If Right(dir1.Path, 1) = "\" Then
            Fname = Dir1.Path & txtFilename
        Else
            Fname = Dir1.Path & "\" & txtFilename
        End If
' get new name and create path-filename
        newname = InputBox("Enter new filename")
        If newname = "" Then Exit Sub            ' leave if new name not supplied
        If Right(dir1.Path, 1) = "\" Then
            newfile = Dir1.Path & newname
        Else
            newfile = Dir1.Path & "\" & newname
        End If
        message = "Rename " & fname & " as " & newname ' confirm
        ans = MsgBox(message, 52)                ' exclamation mark & Yes/No?
        If ans = 6 Then Name fname As newfile
    End If
End Sub
```

10.8 Using the File Selector

With minor amendments, the File Selector form could be incorporated into any other program that needs to find filenames for saving or opening. As an example, let's extend the Draw program, developed in Chapter 7, so that pictures can be saved to and loaded in from disk. The plan is to use the File Selector as the source of the filename, passing it back from there to the Draw form, where it will be used in the save and open routines. We will need to add:

- the File Selector form, with *Rename* and *Quit* replaced by *OK* and *Cancel* buttons;
- a basic module to carry the filename, and a cancel indicator as global variables;
- *Save* and *Open* buttons, with attached code, on the Draw form;
- code to pick up the program flow when it returns from the File Selector form.

Start with the File Selector. If you have not given the Form a name, do so now. You cannot have two called *Form1* in the same project! *frmFile* would be a suitable name.

Open the Draw project, and rename its Form if it is still called *Form1*. I have called mine *frmDraw* – change your code to suit if you use a different name.

Make sure that the **picCanvas** has its **AutoRedraw** property set to *True*. This records any drawing instructions and reruns them if the system needs to rebuild the picture. If AutoRedraw is left at *False* – the default setting – that part of the picture which gets hidden by the File Selector form will be erased.

Use **File | Add File** to bring in the File Selector form.

Set up a basic module with **Insert | Module**.

Edit the File Selector form, *frmFile*, so that the buttons read *OK* and *Cancel*, and replace their existing code with these routines:

```
Sub cmdOK_Click ()
    fname = txtFilename
    frmFile.Hide              ' or whatever your file is called
    frmDraw.Enabled = True    ' see below
    frmDraw.SetFocus          ' or whatever name
End Sub

Sub cmdCancel_Click
    FileIO = True             ' see below
    frmFile.Hide
    frmDraw.Enabled = True
    frmDraw.SetFocus
End Sub
```

Use **Save File As** on the File form, giving it a new filename so that the original form is retained on disk.

We must allow users to abandon an operation – people do change their minds half way through things – but this must not cause a program crash. The solution used here is to have a variable, *FileIO*, which will be set to 0 if the file selection routine is abandoned. The same variable can also be used to signal whether the user is performing a save or an open operation. *FileIO* and the *fname* variable must both exist globally. So, write this into the general area of the basic module:

```
Global fname As String
Global FileIO
```

Save the basic module, giving it a suitable name.

Now back to the Draw form. We want two new buttons on here – you may have to shuffle the existing ones to make space for them. The code for the save operation is split over two procedures – starting on the button's **Click**, and finishing on its **GotFocus**. In between, the program flow passes to the File Selector form.

The design for the routines can be summarised as:

Save button Click

1. Initialise the fname and FileIO variables.
2. Disable the Draw form.
3. Pass the focus to the File Selector, which passes it back to the Save button.

Save button GotFocus

4. If there is no filename, or the routine was abandoned, then exit.
5. Check that the filename has a ".BMP" extension.
6. Save the picture.

The design translates to the code:

```
Private Sub cmdSave_Click()
    fname = ""
    FileIO = 1                          ' starting a save
    frmDraw.Enabled = False
    frmFile.Show
    frmFile.SetFocus
End Sub
```

To save the picture to a file, we can use the **SavePicture** method. This needs to be given the source object (and its Image property), along with a filename. Calling the Refresh method will restore the picture, which will have been partially erased by the File Selector form.

```
Private Sub cmdSave_GotFocus()
    If fname = "" Or FileIO = 0 Then Exit Sub
    If UCase(Right(fname, 4)) <> ".BMP" Then fname = fname & ".BMP"
    SavePicture picCanvas.Image, fname
    picCanvas.Refresh
    FileIO = 0
End Sub
```

The Open operation follows exactly the same pattern, and is again split over the **Click** and **GotFocus** procedures. Don't forget that you can use the Edit Copy and Paste facilities to copy a block of code from one procedure to another.

```
Private Sub cmdOpen_Click()
    fname = ""
    FileIO = 2                          ' starting to open
    frmDraw.Enabled = False
    frmFile.Show
    frmFile.SetFocus
End Sub
```

Notice that the LoadPicture method passes the file to the **Picture** property of the Canvas, though the SavePicture took from the **Image** property.

```
Private Sub cmdOpen_GotFocus()
    If fname = "" Or FileIO = 0 Then Exit Sub
    If UCase(Right(fname, 4)) <> ".BMP" Then fname = fname & ".BMP"
    picCanvas.Picture = LoadPicture(fname)
    picCanvas.Refresh
    FileIO = 0
End Sub
```

Adapting the File Selector form

A little work is needed on the File Selector form. We must set this up so that the program flow returns from here to the appropriate place on the Draw form. This is where the *FileIO* variable earns its keep. It will contain 1 if the File form was activated from a Save routine, and 2 from an Open. We can test the variable, and send the focus back to the cmdSave or cmdOpen button, as appropriate.

```
Private Sub cmdOK_Click()
    fname = File1.Path & "\" & txtFilename
    frmFile.Hide
    frmDraw.Enabled = True
    If FileIO = 1 Then frmDraw.cmdSave.SetFocus
    If FileIO = 2 Then frmDraw.cmdOpen.SetFocus
End Sub
```

10.9 Exercises

1. Design and write a program that uses the internal clock and the Now function to test reaction times. Store the time at the start of the test by the statement *starttime* = *Now*; calculate elapsed time by *elapsed* = *Now* − *starttime*. Note that the value will be a fraction of a day and will have to be multiplied up into seconds.

2. Use a Timer to produce a countdown from 10 down to 1, at one-second intervals.

3. The statement **MkDir** *dir_name* will create a new directory; **RmDir** *dir_name* will remove an (empty) directory; **Kill** *filename* will remove a program; **Name** *old_path&file* **AS** *new_path&file* will move a file from one directory to another; **FileCopy** *old_path&name, new_path&name* will copy a file – between directories if the paths are specified.

    Use these to create a simple file and directory management program. Include confirmation routines for all actions, and test thoroughly within a temporary directory before attempting to use this on any files that might matter!

    Possible solutions to Exercises 1 and 2 are given in Appendix A.

    The files for the *Text Editor* program are available from the Visual Basic page at the author's Web site: http://www.tcp.co.uk/~macbride

11 Sequential files

11.1 Saving data to file

Visual Basic can handle both sequential and random access files.

- A **sequential** file has no particular structure, but consists of a set of data items – of the same or different types – stored in the order in which they were written to the disk. To make sense of the data in the file, it must be read back in the right order, into the right type of variables.

  Sequential files are typically used where there is a mixture of information to be stored, or for permanent storage of data that is held in an array during program run-time. Data files created by word-processors or spreadsheets would normally be stored as sequential files.

- A **random access** file will hold a set of records, each with an identical structure, and each at an identifiable place in the file. If a record's position number is known, it can be read directly from the file, edited and returned to the same place.

  Database management programs normally hold their data in random access files, though if the whole database will fit in memory – and modern machines are well supplied in this respect – a viable alternative is to hold the data in an array and store it on disk as a sequential file.

Using a sequential file

Within a program, files are accessed through a file number. The link between the external (disk) filename and the internal file number is made through the **Open** statement. Its syntax takes the form:

> Open *filename* For *mode* As *#filenumber*

The *filename* is a string expression or variable.

The *modes* are: **Input**, to read from an existing file;

> **Output**, to create a new file, replacing any of the same name;

> **Append**, to add data to the end of an existing file.

The *filenumber* can be given directly. It is usually safe to number the first file you open as 1. If further files are opened while this is still in use, they can then be numbered 2, 3 and so one.

FreeFile

There is a possibility that your file numbers may coincide with others used by other applications in the computer. If you prefer to be sure that there will be no conflict with an existing open file, you can get the number of the next free file handle with the **FreeFile** function, using the line:

> filenum = FreeFile

At the end of the filing session, the link is ended with the Close statement that ensures that all data is written safely to disk. It takes the form:

> Close #filenumber

Writing and Reading Data

Once the file has been opened, data can be written to it with these commands:

Print #filenumber, item, position, item, position,...

Write #filenumber, items

In both cases, there can be any number of items, separated by commas, and they can be any mixture of variables, literal values or functions – in fact, any text that can be printed on screen or paper can be printed to a file.

Print

The **Print** method is designed for use when you are creating files that will later be sent to the printer, e.g. reports from a database. With Print, the dates, numbers and currency are formatted, using the Windows settings on your PC. The layout of text is determined by the *position* value – use a semicolon to place the next item immediately after the last, or **Tab**(*column*) to start the next item at a given column.

If there is any possibility that you may later need to read data back from a Printed file, strings will need special handling. Any that contain commas or newline characters (Chr(13) and Chr(10)), should be enclosed in quotes for reasons that will become clear in a moment.

Write

The **Write** method is the one you should normally use when creating data files to be read by your Basic programs – or by any other database systems. It writes data in the standard comma-separated values format. Numbers and dates are written in their simplest forms, strings are enclosed in quotes, items are separated by commas and a newline character is sent at the end of each Write.

Input

Data·is read back from the file with:

Input #filenumber, variables

The variables must be of the right type and in the right order to match the data file, and the data items must be separated by commas within the file.

Type the following routine into a Form's Click procedure to see the difference between **Write #** and **Print #** in the way they handle strings and commas. It writes a phrase to disk, closes the file, then reopens it, reads the text back in and prints it on the form.

```
Private Sub Form_Click()
    Open "Dolittle" For Output As #1
    phrase = "The rain in Spain, and elsewhere in Iberia, falls mainly on the plain"
    Write #1, phrase
    Close #1
    Open "Dolittle" For Input As #1
    Input #1, instring
    Print  instring
    Close #1
End Sub
```

Click on the form and you should see "The rain in Spain, and elsewhere in Iberia, falls mainly on the plain".

Now replace **Write #1, phrase** with **Print #1, phrase**. Run the program again.

This time, you should see only "The rain in Spain". **Input #** spotted the comma and assumed that it marked the end of the string. If there was a second **Input #** at this point, it would collect "and elsewhere in Iberia".

If you are using Print # to write strings to files, any text containing commas must be explicitly enclosed in quotes. It is often easiest to do this via the ASCII code, as Chr(34). Try it again, this time with the **Print #** line rewritten like this:

```
Print #1, Chr(34) & phrase & chr(34)
```

11.2 Basic filing

This next simple example shows some of the key concepts of handling sequential files. It writes data to a file, reads it back and removes the file from the disk. The file has been named "temp.$$$", which should be sufficiently unusual not to conflict with any files you have already.

To implement it, place three buttons on a new form, and name them *cmdRead*, *cmdWrite* and *cmdRemove*. There are only three procedures, each attached to the appropriate button.

The first, **Write,** creates a telephone contacts list by taking in a series of names and phone numbers and writing them to disk.

```
Private Sub cmdWrite_Click()
    Dim person As String
    Dim telno As String
    Open "temp.$$$" For Output As #1
    Do
        person = InputBox("Name of contact or enter to stop")
        If person = "" Then Exit Do
        telno = InputBox("Tel no")
        Write #1, person, telno
    Loop
    Close #1
End Sub
```

The second, **Read**, inputs the data from the file and prints it on the screen. You will see that the data is read in the same order in which it was written. Try inputting the data the other way round and see what happens.

Notice the test used on the Loop – **Until EOF(1)**. **EOF** is End Of File. This function picks up the code that signals the end of the disk file.

```
Private Sub cmdRead_Click()
    Dim person As String
    Dim telno As String
    Cls
    Open "temp.$$$" For Input As #1
    Do
        Input #1, person, telno
```

```
            Print person, telno
        Loop Until EOF(1)
        Close #1
    End Sub
```

The last, **Remove**, is simply there for tidying purposes – it deletes the file from the disk using the **Kill** statement.

```
    Sub cmdRemove_Click ()
        Kill "temp.$$$"
    End Sub
```

Always use **Kill** with care! It really does delete files – they are not passed to the Recycled Bin in Windows 95, and cannot be recovered unless you can use the MS-DOS **undelete** command.

Task 11.1 Implement the Read & Write program and test it with a variety of data. What difference would it make if the *telno* variable was an Integer?

11.3 Data analysis and storage

This demonstration program performs simple statistical analysis on sets of data, and allows sets to be saved to and loaded in from disk. The analysis is limited to giving the maximum, minimum, total and mean values. All are produced and displayed together. If you wrote the data analysis program set as an exercise in Chapter 5, you could use that as the base of this example. There are five procedures in the program, run from a simple menu.

```
    File            Data
        Save            Create
        Open            Analyse
        Quit
```

The sets can be of any size as the dimension of the *dataset* array is determined by the user when creating each new set. The undimensioned array is set up at the general level, along with a *MaxNumber* variable which will be used to store the size.

```
    general declarations
        Dim dataset() As Integer        ' undimensioned array
        Dim MaxNumber As Integer
```

The **Create** routine starts by asking the user for the number of elements in the set, then dimensions the array with the **ReDim** statement. Note that this subtracts 1 from *MaxNumber*, on the assumption that if someone asks for 10 elements, they do want 10, and **Dim dataset(10)** would create an array of 11 elements, numbered 0 to 10. The data values are then collected – InputBox is used throughout, as it provides the simplest method of getting values.

```
    Private Sub mnuCreate_Click ()
        MaxNumber = InputBox("Maximum number of elements?")
        ReDim dataset(MaxNumber - 1)
        For element = 0 To MaxNumber - 1
```

```
        dataset(element) = InputBox("Enter data for element no " & element)
    Next element
End Sub
```

Ideally, there should be another routine to edit or add data to the set, but I'm trying to keep things simple. Your users will just have to get it right first time!

The **Analysis** should be self-explanatory, though you might note the use of the variable *NewLine* to hold characters 13 and 10 – the two that produce the carriage return and line feed. These improve the readability of the routine that creates the four-line message.

```
Private Sub mnuAnalyse_Click ()
    NewLine = Chr(13) & Chr(10)
    Max = dataset(0)
    Min = dataset(0)
    total = dataset(0)
    For element = 1 To MaxNumber - 1
        If dataset(element) > Max Then Max = dataset(element)
        If dataset(element) < Min Then Min = dataset(element)
        total = total + dataset(element)
    Next element
    mean = total / (MaxNumber)
    message = "Total = " & total & NewLine
    message = message & "Mean = " & mean & NewLine
    message = message & "Maximum = " & Max & NewLine
    message = message & "Minimum = " & Min
    MsgBox message
End Sub
```

The **Save** routine uses an InputBox to get a filename – a crude method which you may prefer to replace with the File Selector form. When we write the data to file, we must

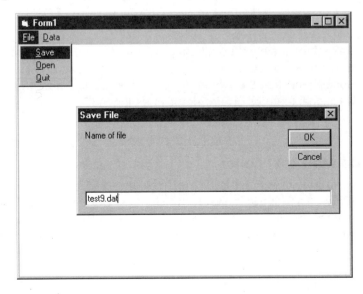

Figure 11.1 A composite screenshot to show the File menu and InputBox.

think ahead to what will happen when it is read back in. The array will have to be ReDimensioned for the incoming data, which means that the program will need to know the size of the array before it starts to read its data. The solution is to write MaxNumber as the first value on the file.

```
Private Sub mnuSave_Click()
    filename = InputBox("Name of file ", "Open file")
    Open filename For Output As #1
    Write #1, MaxNumber
    For element = 0 To MaxNumber - 1
        Write #1, dataset(element)
    Next element
    Close #1
End Sub
```

The Open and Input code can be created by copying and editing the Save routine, as the two can be very similar. You will need to add the **ReDim** line, and replace **For Output** and **Write #** by **For Input** and **Input#**.

```
Private Sub mnuOpen_Click()
    filename = InputBox("Name of file ", "Open file")
    Open filename For Input As #1
    Input #1, MaxNumber
    ReDim dataset(MaxNumber - 1)
    For element = 0 To MaxNumber - 1
        Input #1, dataset(element)
    Next element
    Close #1
End Sub
```

The **For** loop handles the Input well here, as we know the number of items to be read. As we saw in the last example, where there is an unknown quantity of data on the file, we can use a loop that checks for the End Of File, with the **EOF** function:

Task 11.2 Take the simple data analysis program that you developed earlier and add these new objects and procedures to it. Test each new procedure as it is added, and test the whole program thoroughly when it is complete. What additional features or error-traps does it need?

11.4 The Extended Text Editor

This second example of sequential filing demonstrates the transfer of data between controls and files. To produce it, start with the Text Editor program and add to it the File Selector form and a basic module, as shown with the Draw program at the end of the last chapter. Edit the editor form to add *Save* and *Open* to the *File* menu.

Program flow

Transferring control to the File form is handled in a slightly different way here – if only to show that there are always alternatives. In the *Save/Open* routines on the main

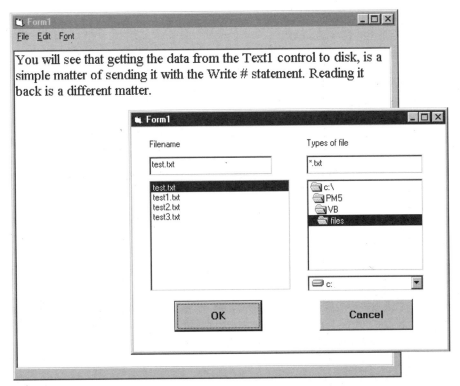

Figure 11.2 The file selector form pulled up in front of the editor.

form, execution starts in the **Click** procedure, transfers to the File Selector form, then returns to the **GotFocus** procedures of the buttons. We cannot use that technique here as menu items do not have a **GotFocus** procedure.

The routines start in the same way as in the Draw program. They initialise the *fname* and *FileIO* variables, disable the editing form and pull up the File Selector form.

```
Private Sub mnuSave_Click()
    fname = ""
    FileIO = 1
    frmEdit.Enabled = False
    frmFile.Show
    frmFile.SetFocus
End Sub
Private Sub mnuOpen_Click()
    fname = ""
    FileIO = 2
    frmEdit.Enabled = False
    frmFile.Show
    frmFile.SetFocus
End Sub
```

You will probably need to adapt the routine on the File Selector form that returns control to the Editor – if only to change the form names.

The *OK* button code should look like this:

```
Private Sub cmdOK_Click()
    fname = File1.Path & "\" & txtFilename
    frmFile.Hide
    frmEdit.Enabled = True
    frmEdit.SetFocus
End Sub
```

This time the return from the File Selector form is picked up in the **GotFocus** procedure of the *Text1* TextBox. The routine is more complex that the earlier ones because there is only one block of code, and it is in a procedure which is executed whenever the TextBox comes into focus – wherever it was before. It has to deal with three situations:

- a save has started;
- an open has started;
- no file operations are active.

Note:	The code would have worked just as well written into the **Activate** procedure of the form, but *not* into the form's **GotFocus** procedure. If a form contains controls, the focus returns to one of those and not to the form itself.

Before we look at these routines, let's turn for a moment to the problems of saving formatted text.

Text and font settings on file

Saving text is slightly more complicated than saving a picture, especially if you also want to save the font settings – which we do.

The font data can be written to the disk with **Write #**, and can go either before or after the text. The order in which the settings are written is also irrelevant, as long as we use exactly the same order when reading them back in. They could have been written as a comma-separated list in a single statement. Printing each one individually makes it more readable and easier to check that the Open routine follows the same order.

Reading the font settings back is more complex than writing them. Visual Basic will not allow you to Input values directly to the properties of controls. To get them there, we must take them into a variable, then transfer from that to the property. It's a roundabout way of doing things, but it works.

```
Private Sub Text1_GotFocus()
    If fname = "" Or FileIO = 0 Then Exit Sub
    filenum = FreeFile

    If FileIO = 1 Then
    ' save operation in progress
        Open fname For Output As #filenum
        Write #filenum, Text1.FontBold
        Write #filenum, Text1.FontItalic
        Write #filenum, Text1.FontSize
```

```
        Write #filenum, Text1.FontName
        Write #filenum, Text1.Text
        Close #filenum

    Elself FilelO = 2 Then
    ' open operation in progress
        Open fname For Input As #filenum
        Input #filenum, temp
        Text1.FontBold = temp
        Input #filenum, temp
        Text1.FontItalic = temp
        Input #filenum, temp
        Text1.FontSize = temp
        Input #filenum, temp
        Text1.FontName = temp
        Input #filenum, temp
        Text1.Text = temp
        Close #filenum
    End If
End Sub
```

Notice the second line of this routine:

```
    filenum = FreeFile
```

The FreeFile function checks your system to find the next available stream number. In practice, in this program, **filenum = 1** would work just as well, as you can only ever have one file open at a time. The use of the FreeFile function is essential where several files can be open at the same time.

11.5 Exercises

1. Option buttons provide a convenient way of handling responses to multiple-choice tests, for their captions can display the alternative answers and only one can be selected. Design and implement a program which will read a file containing questions, answers and the right answer, taking one question at a time and displaying it with a set of option buttons. The file itself can be created in Write or any word-processor that can output an ASCII text file.

2. Payroll programs often store their data in sequential files, as every record is accessed at each payrun. Write a program to manage a simplified system. It must have routines to add and remove employees, as well as to calculate and print the weekly payslips. The file should contain the employee's name, reference number, hourly rate, tax code, total earnings for the year to date and total tax paid to date. When calculating the week's pay, assume that the first 37 hours are paid at the normal rate and additional hours at time and a half.

   A possible solution to Exercise 11.1 is given in Appendix A; a solution for Exercise 11.2 is included in the Lecturer's Supplement disk.

12 Records and random access files

12.1 Record structures

Record structures can be used in many situations where it is useful to keep items of data together, but their most prominent use is in association with random access files In Visual Basic you can define your own record structures, in the same way that you can with RECORD in Pascal. Of course, being Visual Basic, it gives you far more flexibility and a far wider range of data types than you get with Pascal, but we won't go into the more exotic parts in this slim book. Record structures are defined by the **Type** statement, and must be written into the general declarations area of a basic module. You cannot define a Type in a form, though once the type is defined, you can declare variables of that type in any form within the same project. Definition takes the form:

```
Type type_name
    var_name As data_type
    var_name As data_type
    ....
End Type
```

The definition of the subordinate variables (the *fields*) within the record follows the normal rules for variable declaration, with one significant exception – the lengths of strings must be specified. This gives the records a fixed size, which is needed when allocating space in memory or on disk.

For example, if you were creating a student database, and wanted to hold the name, phone number, fees, and end-of-year results for each student, the record structure might be defined by:

```
Type StudentRecord
    FullName As String * 30   ' specifies length of string
    TelNo As String * 12
    Fees As Currency
    Marks(10) As Integer
End Type
```

This allocates 30 characters for the name and 12 for the phone number – before deciding on these limits, the wise designer would have taken a sample of the data to be stored and found the longest items in each string field. Note that *Marks()* is an array. You can have arrays *within* records and you can have arrays *of* records.

Variables of the new type can be declared on the module or on any forms within the project.

```
Dim Student As StudentRecord
Dim Class(30) As StudentRecord
```

The first line sets up a variable to hold the details of one student; the second sets up an array of 31 (0 to 30) record structures.

Within the code, you can treat the whole of the data in a record as a single unit when copying it to another variable of the same type:

Class(element) = Student

A record can also be written to, and read from, disk by the **Put** and **Get** statements (see Section 2, below). Both of these handle whole records as units, transferring all the fields in one operation. When you want to input data, or display it, whether by Print or through a control, it must be done by individual fields, identifying them by their record variable and field name, separated by a full stop.

Print Student.FullName

Student.Fees = CCur(InputBox("Enter Fees Paid"))

When you are working with arrayed records or arrays within records, the identification can get long-winded:

Class(StudentNo).Marks(AssNo) = txtMarks.Text

Here we have an array of records called *Class*; *StudentNo* identifies the individual within the class. One of the fields in the record is *Marks*, and *AssNo* holds the number of the assignment.

12.2 Random access files

Opening a file for random access follows the pattern for sequential files, with two significant variations.

- With sequential files you can only read from or write to them at any one time, so they must be opened either for Input or Output. Random access files can be read and written at the same time, and they are simply opened **For Random**.

- The second point to note with these, is that the system needs to know the size of the record structure, so that it knows how to organise the disk space. The **Len = reclen** phrase at the end of the statement gives this information. This should not be confused with the **Len()** function, which returns the number of bytes in a string – or in a record – and which is often used alongside its namesake in the Open line. For example:

Open "student.dat" For Random As #Fnum Len = Len(student)

This sets up a link with a file called "student.dat" – creating a new one if there is no matching file there at the time. The size of each record will be the total number of bytes in the *student* type.

Get

Records are read with the **Get** statement. It is given the filenumber, the position of the record in the file, and the name of the variable into which data is to be copied.

Get Fnum, RecNum, Student

This will copy the data in the file linked to *Fnum*, from record number *RecNum* into the variable *Student*. Trying to read beyond the end of the file will produce an error.

Put

Writing to the file is handled by the **Put** statement, which follows the same pattern.

Put Fnum, RecNum, Student

This would replace any existing data at record number *RecNum*, or create a new record at that position.

Seek

Positioning in the file can also be handled by the **Seek** function and the **Seek** statement. Of the two, the function is probably more useful.

> **RecNum = Seek(Fnum)**
>
> ....
>
> **Seek Fnum, RecNum**
> **Get Fnum, , Student**

The first line will pass to *RecNum* the position of the next record in the file linked by *Fnum*. The second sets the file pointer to the *RecNum* position in the file. Note that in the Get after the Seek statement, the position number is omitted, as the positioning has already been taken care of.

One last function to note, before moving on to an example, is **LOF()**. This returns the Length Of a File, and can be used in conjunction with *Len()* to work out how many records there are in a file:

> **NumberOfRecords = LOF(Fnum) \ Len(Record)**

12.3 The staff database

Students are often asked to write student database programs. I thought it would make a change to design one to handle the lecturing staff.

With any database program the design must start from the data itself – what do we want to store, and what do we want to get out of it?

The nature of the data

For each member of staff we will hold:

Name (Surname & Initials only)	20 characters will be enough
Reference Number	which can also be the record number
Department	10 characters will cope with the longest
Grade	a simple integer
Teaching Hours	may contain fractions

From this we can derive the Type definition that will be written into the linked module:

> **Type lecturer**
>   **Refno As Long**   ' index numbers must be Long
>   **LName As String * 20**   ' cannot use Name – it is a reserved word
>   **Dept As String * 10**
>   **Grade As Integer**
>   **Hours As Single**
> **End Type**

As the data is held on file, and each record can be accessed when wanted, there is no need for any global variables, and only a few, to handle the file itself, are needed at the general level. The whole code for the general declarations procedure is then:

> **general declarations**
>   **Type lecturer**
>   **Refno As Long**
>   **LName As String * 20**

```
          Dept As String * 10
          Grade As Integer
          Hours As Single
       End Type
       Dim staff As lecturer          ' record variable
       Dim Fnum As Integer
       Dim RecCount As Long
       Dim Fnum As Integer
```

This gives us a record variable called *staff*, with the fields *staff.RefNo*, *staff.LName*, *staff.Dept*, *staff.Grade* and *staff.Hours*.

Desired outputs

We will want to be able to:

1. Display the details of any individual and of all lecturers.

    If the main form is laid out to display one record, we can have routines that will step forwards and backwards through it.

    An alternative 'Table View' form can display all records – though this quick and easy solution will not work if there are more records than will fill a form.

2. To keep the database up to date, we must be able to add, delete and edit records. If Text Boxes are used for the display of data, their built-in editing facilities will do away with the need for a special edit routine.

3. New and edited records should be saved before they are removed from the screen. This could be handled through a button marked Save, but it would also be a good idea to include a save operation at the start of other routines, in case the user forgets to click the button.

4. Print details of one or all lecturers. The *PrintForm* method can be used to copy the individual form and table view to paper.

5. Find any individual, searching either by name or reference number.

6. Select groups, based on either their department or grade.

The record structure determines the nature of the data entry / display / edit form. The reference number can be worked into the form's Caption. The cmdSave button is only visible during the Add procedure.

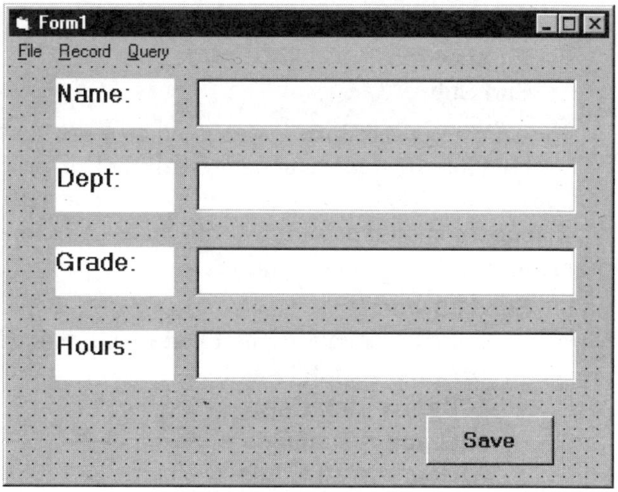

Figure 12.1 The staff database form.

133

The operations that will lead us to these desired outputs can be translated to a set of commands and a menu structure:

File	Record	Query
View Table	Add	Find
Print	Delete	By Name
This Record	Next	By Number
Print All Records	Previous	Select
Exit		By Department
		By Grade

In a program like this, where each procedure stands largely by itself, linked to others only through the common data file, it is simplest to discuss the design and coding of each separately.

12.4 Design and coding

Initialisation

This is best done in the **Form Load** procedure, which will be executed as soon as the program starts. Initialisation operations are:

open the connection to the data file;
find out how many records there are on disk;
pick up the first one;
if the file is being accessed for the first time,
   allocate a reference number for the first record;
display the record on screen

As we will want an identical display routine at several points in the program, it makes sense to set this up as a separate procedure. Here's the main part of the initialisation:

```
Private Sub Form_Load ()
    Fnum = FreeFile
    Open "Staff.dta" For Random As #Fnum Len = Len(staff)
    RecCount = LOF(Fnum) / Len(staff)
    Get Fnum, 1, staff                         ' open at first record - if any
    If RecCount = 0 Then staff.RefNo = 1
    showrec
End Sub
```

The *showrec* procedure is designed to work on the current record, so that must be selected and its data read before calling this procedure. It will copy the fields into the appropriate Text Boxes on the Form. The reference number must not be open to change, so should be written into a Label or combined with a little heading text and made into the Form's Caption.

```
Sub showrec ()
    Form1.Caption = "Staff Database. Rec No: " & staff.RefNo
    txtName = staff.Lname
    txtDept = staff.Dept
    txtGrade = staff.Grade
    txtHour = staff.Hours
End Sub
```

Display / Edit Controls

The main form will need code to pick up any changes made to the displayed data. It is not enough to merely copy the values from the Text boxes.

- The *Grade* and *Hours* must be converted from Variants to a numeric values before passing to the record's fields, or there will be a 'Wrong data type' error.
- The *Name* and *Dept* could be copied straight to the fields, but it is best to remove any leading spaces first, using the **Trim** function. Spaces creep in all too easily and will affect the table view. More importantly, they will make search operations more difficult.

If we can run these operations from the Change events of the Text boxes we will be sure of picking up all edits.

```
Private Sub txtName_Change ()
    staff.Lname = Trim(NameBox)
End Sub

Private Sub txtDept_Change ()
    staff.Dept = Trim(Deptbox)
End Sub

Private Sub txtGrade_Change ()
    staff.Grade = Val(GradeBox)
End Sub

Private Sub txtHour_Change ()
    staff.Hours = Val(HourBox)
End Sub
```

12.5 Record menu options

The *Add*, *Next* and *Previous* procedures will all start by writing the current record to disk, so that any changes made to the current record are stored before another record is read in or created. (To guarantee that all data is always retained, we should write the same **Put** line into the start of *all* procedures. It has been omitted from many here in the interests of brevity.)

The Add routine can be called up at any point, though all new records are added at the end of the file.

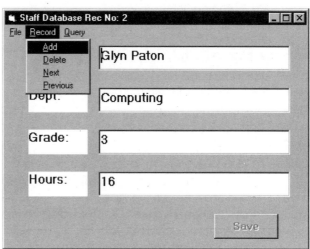

Figure 12.2 The data entry/edit form in use.

Add

The **Add** procedure must set up a new record, by allocating a reference/record number and clearing the *staff* variable of the current values, and ensure that the data is saved to disk. The current record is saved at the start, in case there have been any changes.

The reference number is found by adding one to the record count, so the new record always goes at the end of the file. The saving is managed by making the *cmdSave* button visible, and attaching a **Put** line to this.

```
Private Sub mnuAdd_Click ()
      Put Fnum, staff.RefNo, staff           ' write current record to disk
      cmdSave.Enabled = True                 ' turn on the Save button
      RecCount = RecCount + 1                 ' one more record
      staff.RefNo = RecCount                  ' create its reference number
      staff.Lname = ""                        ' clear out old data
      staff.Dept = ""
      staff.Grade = 0
      staff.Hours = 0
      showrec                                 ' update the form display
End Sub

Private Sub cmdSave_Click ()
      Put Fnum, staff.RefNo, staff           ' save the new record
      cmdSave.Enabled = False                 ' turn off the button
End Sub
```

Delete

The **Delete** procedure, as implemented here, merely blanks out the data, allowing the reference number to be reused for another person. It does not actually remove the record. The 'Deleted' records are marked by "Blank" in the *Lname* field. A check for this in the Print procedure stops such records from being displayed. The person maintaining the database could look for a Blank record, and overwrite that, when entering the new details for a new member of staff.

```
Private Sub mnuDelete_Click ()
      staff.Lname = "Blank"
      staff.Dept = ""
      staff.Grade = 0
      staff.Hours = 0
      Put Fnum, staff.RefNo, staff
      showrec
End Sub
```

Note: Visual Basic offers no simple way to delete a record from a random access disk file. We could close up the gaps left by deletions by reading in all the records one at a time, writing valid ones to a new file and replacing the old file with the new, slimmer version. As this would change the reference numbers, it is not a perfect solution, but you may like to write a CleanFile routine that would do this. For more efficient random access file handling, you really have to start indexing them, but this is beyond the scope of this book.

Next

In the **Next** procedure, we can use the **Seek()** function to move on to the next record, checking that there is one before attempting to display it, and giving a 'No More Records' message at the end of the file.

```
Private Sub mnuNext_Click ()
    Put Fnum, staff.RefNo, staff          ' store current record
    temp = Seek(Fnum)                     ' find the next
    If temp <= RecCount Then               ' check for the end
        Get Fnum, temp, staff
    Else MsgBox "No More Records ", 64
    End If
    showrec
End Sub
```

Previous

With the **Previous** procedure, we cannot Seek backwards, but we can use the current record's reference number to calculate the position of the previous record. Here we must look for the start of the file, and avoid stepping backwards into oblivion.

```
Private Sub mnuPrevious_Click ()
    Put Fnum, staff.RefNo, staff
    temp = staff.RefNo - 1                 ' find previous number
    If temp > 0 Then                       ' check for the beginning
        Get Fnum, temp, staff
    Else MsgBox "Start of File ", 64
    End If
    showrec
End Sub
```

12.6 File menu options

View Table

The **View Table** procedure will bring a second form into view and print headings and the details of all records on it. This second form can be blank, except for a *Done* button which will carry code to tuck the form out of sight when the user has finished with it. On return to the main form, we should display the same record that was there when we left it, so we must retain its reference number and *Get* it back at the end.

- If you wanted, you could disable or hide the data entry/edit form while the table is displayed. To do this, write a **Hide** line in the **mnuView** procedure, and add a matching **Show** line to the Done button on the table's form.

As we shall also want identical headings and record printing routines for the Select options, it would be useful to make these into procedures, (*viewheads* and *viewrec*) which could be called from all options. This is true even for *viewrec*, though it consists of only one line. In any one program, you should not have to write the same code more than once.

```
Private Sub mnuView_Click ()
    temp = staff.RefNo              ' store current record number
    viewheads
    For n = 1 To RecCount
        Get Fnum, n, staff          ' Get and Print all records
        viewrec
    Next n
    Get Fnum, temp, staff           ' return to previous place
    showrec
End Sub

Sub viewheads ()
    Form2.Visible = True
    Form2.SetFocus
    Form2.Cls
    Form2.Print "RefNo"; Tab(10); "Name "; Tab(30); "Dept"; Tab(50); "Grade";
        Tab(60); "Hours"                        ' all one long line
End Sub

Sub viewrec ()
    Form2.Print staff.RefNo; Tab(10); staff.Lname; Tab(30); staff.Dept; Tab(50);
        staff.Grade; Tab(60); staff.Hours       ' all one long line
End Sub
```

The **Done** button simply tucks away the table view form. If you decide to hide or disable the data entry/edit form, bring it back into play in this procedure.

```
Private Sub cmdDone_Click ()
    Form2.Visible = False           ' put it away
End Sub
```

Print

With the two **Print** procedures, that for a single record does no more than send the form to the printer. The one to print all the records is based on the *mnuView* procedure with two changes. Output is directed to the *printer* object, and a check for 'Blank' as a name cuts out the display of deleted records. This same check could be written into *mnuView* if desired.

- The **RTrim** function in the check line is essential. String fields in record types have fixed length, and are padded out with spaces from the end of their actual text. "Blank" does not match "Blank ". The solution to this problem lies in **RTrim()** which trims off spaces to the right of the text.

```
Private Sub mnuPrintThis_Click ()
    Form1.PrintForm
End Sub

Private Sub mnuPrintAll_Click ()
    printer.Print "RefNo"; Tab(10); "Name " Tab(30); "Dept"; Tab(40); "Grade";
        Tab(50); "Hours"                        ' all one long line
    For n = 1 To RecCount
        Get Fnum, n, staff
```

```
        If RTrim(staff.Lname) <> "Blank" Then
            printer.Print staff.RefNo; Tab(10); staff.Lname; Tab(30); staff.Dept;
                Tab(40); staff.Grade; Tab(50); staff.Hours    ' one long line
        End If
    Next n
    printer.EndDoc
End Sub
```

Exit

When the program is closed down with the **Exit** option, the current record is written and the file closed to ensure that all data is safely on the disk.

```
Private Sub mnuExit_Click ()
    Put Fnum, staff.RefNo, staff        ' save changes to current
    Close Fnum
    End
End Sub
```

12.7 Find and Select

Find by Number

This is simply a matter of taking a record number, checking that is it valid, and Seeking to that place on the disk.

InputBox and MsgBox are used to get the target in and a message out. You may prefer to replace these quick but crude boxes with something more sophisticated, once you have got the main routines working properly.

```
Private Sub mnuFindNum_Click ()
    Dim target As Long
    target = InputBox("Enter Reference Number", "Find")
    If target > 0 And target <= RecCount Then
        Seek Fnum, target
        Get Fnum, , staff
        showrec
    Else MsgBox "Record " & target & " not present ", 48
    End If
End Sub
```

Find by Name

Finding **By Name**, or by any other value held in a field, is a little more complicated. We can do it by reading through the file, comparing the target value with that of each record in turn until a match is found, or the end of the file is reached.

Note that *RTrim* is used again. The target value, whether held in a normal String or Variant variable, will not be padded to the same length as the stored values, so that even if the names look the same to you, they won't to the system. The design can be summarised:

```
    set Found to false
    get target value
    loop through file
```

```
                    if matching value found
                         display record
                         set Found to true
                         exit from the loop
                    if found still false at the end
                         display Not Found message
```

This translates directly to the code:

```
Private Sub mnuFindName_Click ()
    Dim target As String
    Dim Found
    Found = False
    target = InputBox("Enter Target Name", "Find")
    For n = 1 To RecCount
        Get Fnum, n, staff
        If target = RTrim(staff.Lname) Then          ' note the trimming
            showrec
            Found = True  ' signal success
            Exit For
        End If
    Next n
    If Not Found Then MsgBox "Record " & target & " not present", 48
End Sub
```

Select

The two **Select** procedures both follow the same pattern as *Find By Name*, but adjusted to cope with the fact that they are hunting for sets of matching records, rather than an individual one. Instead of stopping when a matching record is found and displaying it, all matching records are printed on the table view form. The *Found* variable is used here to keep a count of the matches.

- Note how the *viewheads* and *viewrec* procedures are pushed into service again. This doesn't just save typing, it also means that any improvements to the display only have to be done once.

```
Private Sub mnuSelectDept_Click ()
    Dim target As String
    Dim Found As Integer

    Found = 0
    target = InputBox("Which Department", "Select")
    viewheads
    For n = 1 To RecCount
        Get Fnum, n, staff
        If target = RTrim(staff.Dept) Then
            viewrec
            Found = Found + 1
        End If
    Next n
```

```
    If Found = 0 Then
        MsgBox "No matching records", 48
    Else Form2.Print Chr(10); Found; " Records"
    End If
End Sub
```

mnuSelectGrade is very similar. Copy-and-Paste, then edit to create this code.

```
Private Sub mnuSelectGrade_Click ()
    Dim target As Integer
    Dim Found As Integer

    Found = 0
    target = InputBox("Which Grade", "Select")
    viewheads
    For n = 1 To RecCount
        Get Fnum, n, staff
        If target = staff.Grade Then
            viewrec
            Found = Found + 1
        End If
    Next n

    If Found = 0 Then
        MsgBox "No matching records", 48
    Else Form2.Print Chr(10); Found; " Records"
    End If
End Sub
```

12.8 Exercises

1. Working from the fragments given at the start of this chapter, write a program to handle student records, using a random access file for storage. The program should offer the same range of facilities as that in the Staff Database, plus routines to display total and average marks.

2. A pocket diary is a form of random access database, and one that can be implemented readily in Visual Basic. The functions that convert Dates to numbers and vice versa, can be used to turn diary dates into record numbers, using statements like:

    RecNo = DateValue(GivenDate) - DateValue("31/12/94")

    This would produce record numbers for a 1995 diary. *GivenDate* must be in a suitable form and include the year number. As a similar expression can convert record numbers back into dates, you will not need to store dates in the records.

    Possible solutions for Exercises 1 and 2 are included in the Lecturer's Supplement disk.

    The files for the Staff database program are available from the Visual Basic page at the author's Web site: http://www.tcp.co.uk/~macbride

13 Graphics(2)

Time for a little fun and to get further into graphics by trying our hand at animation and writing a graphic game.

13.1 Working with imported graphics

We first met the idea of assigning graphics to the Picture property of controls back in Chapter 3, and have touched on it a few times since. It's time now to explore rather more deeply into the possibilities of graphics in Visual Basic programs.

Controls for graphics

Four types of control have Picture properties into which graphics can be imported:

- In a **Form**, a graphic can act as a background or a decoration. The image will appear with its top left corner in the top left corner of the form. If it is smaller than the form, it will be surrounded by white space; if larger, the form's scroll bars can be turned on to allow access to the off-form parts.

- In a **PictureBox**, if the *AutoSize* property is set to True, the box will adjust to fit the graphic exactly. Drawn graphics can be added to the imported picture if wanted. As a Picture box can be smaller than its enclosing form and can be moved during run-time, it can be used for animation.

- An **Image** handles imported graphics in the same way as a Picture box, but as this is a simpler control it takes less memory and is manipulated more quickly by the system during execution. For these reasons, Images are the prime choice for animation.

- The **OLE control** can also take graphics, and its OLE link means that the graphic can be changed, via its original program, during run-time. The OLE control could be used where you want to view and edit graphics. Object Linking and Embedding is a complex process, and is beyond the scope of this book.

Most other controls have *DragIcon* properties which can hold Icon images, to be displayed when the control is moved during run time.

Loading pictures

Forms, Picture boxes and Images can pick up their graphics during runtime with the LoadPicture() function. Its syntax is:

control.Picture = LoadPicture(*filename*)

This guarantees that the imported graphic is the latest image, but loading from disk takes time. Time is, of course, a key factor in animation, but unnecessary delays should be avoided wherever possible and there are two techniques that can help here.

With all three controls, the graphic can be linked to – and displayed in – the control during design time, by clicking on its Picture property. This brings up an Open File dialog box through which a file can be selected. The graphic is incorporated into the program file, and will remain the same even if the original is updated. If you do edit the graphic, you will have to go back and reload its file. These three can also take their images from the Picture properties of other controls. If all the graphics that are wanted in a program are loaded into a set of (invisible) Images at design time, they can be copied from there to the appropriate (visible) control when needed during the run. This gives us the quickest and simplest way of changing the picture in a control.

Graphics files

The graphics imported into Pictures can be .BMP or .DIB (BitMaPs), .RLE (RunLength Encoded), .WMF (Windows MetaFile) or .ICO (ICOns). Bitmaps are probably the simplest to use, as these are the default file types for Paintbrush, which is presumably where you will be creating your graphics.

13.2 Animation

This next example is ridiculous, trivial and not to be missed. Animation is such a rewarding activity that it drives you to explore deeper into the system in search of better effects. Get this program running, embellish it and extend it, and you will find that you have learnt far more than you would have expected about the interaction between controls and events. As shown here, the program makes a stick man run backwards and forwards across the screen. The animation is crude – but that is merely a reflection of my limitations as an artist. The images that you animate will be ones that you have created yourself, and they can be as colourful and detailed as you like.

Before you can do anything else, you must create a set of graphics to animate. Five are needed for this simple animation – two facing left, two facing right and one standing still. This is an absolute minimum. For smoother movement you need at least three or four images for each step. When the core program is running properly, you might like to extend it to add a third or fourth graphic for each direction. Each picture should be the same size, and no larger than needed – the larger the graphic, the slower the animation.

The simplest way to achieve this is to draw one man in Paint, select an area which just encloses him and save it to file with **Edit | Copy To**.

Next, open that file, edit it to create the next image and save it with a new name.

Do the same for the other three graphics.

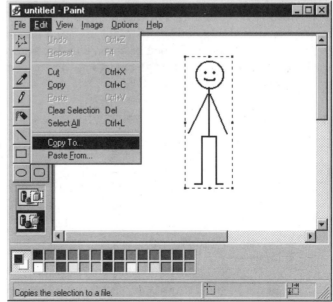

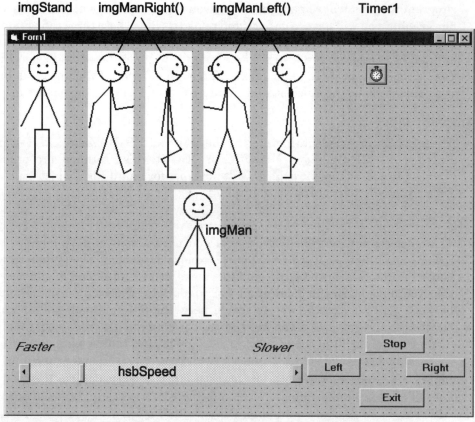

Figure 13.1 The animation form showing the active controls.

imgStore, imgRight, imgLeft and imgMan are Images, whose Picture properties
have been set to bitmap graphics produced by Paint.

Basic techniques

The animation is handled by copying graphics from the invisible stores into one visible
Image, alternating between two pictures and moving the Image at the same time. A
variable, *Manstep*, is flipped between 0 and 1, and serves to index the control arrays,
ManLeft and *ManRight*, that hold the alternative pictures.

```
If Manstep = 0 Then
    Manstep = 1
Else
    Manstep = 0
End If
....
imgMan.Picture = imgManLeft(Manstep).Picture
```

This could easily be extended if there were more than two pictures for each direction.
With three alternative images, you would want this:

```
Manstep = ManStep + 1
If Manstep > 2 Then Manstep = 0
....
imgMan.Picture = imgManLeft(Manstep).Picture
```

How far to move with each new image depends upon the size and nature of the image. As developed here, where my Man's step is around 400 Twips, an adjustment of 200 to the Left property produces a reasonable effect. Trial and error is the best way forward.

The whole of the movement routine is run off a Timer. This gives us continuous movement, no matter what else is happening on the form, plus an easy way of adjusting the speed, by linking the Timer Interval to the Scroll Bar.

Form layout

Where you place controls on this form is very much a matter of individual choice, and the location of some controls is quite irrelevant. Those images that are used to store graphics can be anywhere at all – even on top of each other if you want to save space. You will need five of these, called *imgStand*, *imgManLeft(0)* and *(1)*, *imgManRight(0)* and *(1)*.

The Scroll Bar should be set up to range from a Min of 5 or so to a Max of 500. The value from here will be passed to the Timer's Interval. Anything more than 500 (half a second) would be just too slow. The Timer is initially turned off. It is enabled by clicking on the *cmdLeft* and *cmdRight* buttons.

The Animation code

```
general declarations
    Dim Manstep As Integer
    Dim Way As String
Private Sub Form_Load ()
    Manstep = 0
    Way = "None"                       ' not going anywhere
End Sub
Private Sub cmdLeft_Click ()
    Way = "Left"                       ' turn left
    Timer1.Enabled = True              ' and go
End Sub
Private Sub cmdRight_Click ()
    Way = "Right"                      ' turn right
    Timer1.Enabled = True              ' and go
End Sub
Private Sub hsbSpeed_Change ()
    Timer1.Interval = hsbSpeed.Value   ' copy value from scroll bar to timer
End Sub
Private Sub Timer1_Timer ()
    If Manstep = 0 Then                ' flip alternate image variable
        Manstep = 1
    Else
        Manstep = 0
    End If
    If run = "Left" Then
        imgMan.Left = imgMan.Left - 100 ' move left
```

```
            imgMan.Picture = imgManLeft(Manstep).Picture      ' new left picture
        Else
            imgMan.Left = imgMan.Left + 100                    ' move right
            imgMan.Picture = imgManRight(Manstep).Picture      ' new right picture
        End If
    End Sub
    Private Sub StopBtn_Click ()
        timer1.Enabled = False                                 ' stop moving
        imgMan.Picture = imgStand.Picture                      ' standing picture
    End Sub
    Private Sub cmdExit_Click ()
        End
    End Sub
```

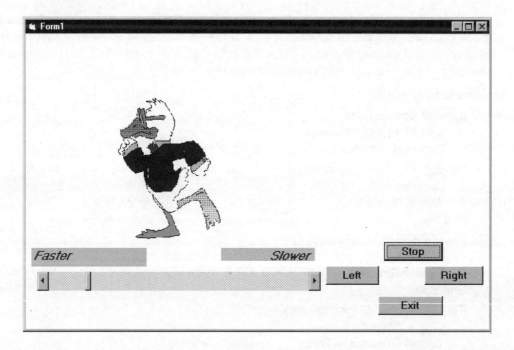

Figure 13.2 And when you've got it going, do replace those stick men with some pictures with a bit more style!

Task 13.1 Create your own set of pictures and animate them as described above. Once you have the program working at this simple level, either add Up and Down controls, or adapt it to produce smoother movement. What would you have to do to give the character a life of its own, so that it could move without being controlled by buttons?

13.3 DIY Minesweeper!

I find that games are as good a spur as animation for making me learn more about a programming language. The search for that elusive quality of playability is a hard taskmaster. The screen layout and the control system must be clean and clear; movement and changes to stationary screens should be smooth and slick; crash-proofing should be as complete as can be, extending to 'idiot-proofing' (guarding against actions that you cannot imagine anyone would ever attempt.) Having set such high standards, I am reluctant to put the next offering forward, but it must be done.

This next is program based on the excellent and addictive Minesweeper games that Microsoft supply as part of the Windows package. (If you have never played it, do so now. It is an essential piece of research and preparation for this program.) Briefly, the nature of the game is this.

The board is a grid of tiles, beneath some of which lurk mines. You click with the left button on a tile if you think there is no mine beneath it. At first you can only stab at random, and if you are wrong, you are blown up. If there is no mine, the tile is removed to display the number of mines in adjacent squares. If there are no adjacent mines, the system checks each of the surrounding squares, as if they had been clicked, clearing back the covering tiles until numbered squares are found. This runs recursively, clearing around every blank, until you have an area of blanks with an edging of

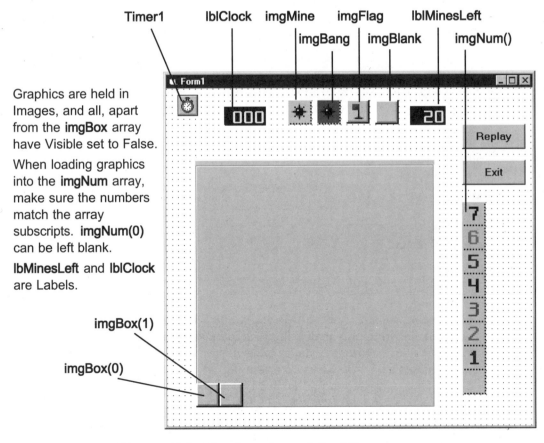

Figure 13.3 The form layout for Minesweeper.

numbered squares indicating mines beyond. When you think you have located a mine, a click with the right button places a flag on that square. (There is also a routine to deal with simultaneous left and right clicks, which we will ignore.) To win, you have to flag all the mines and clear all the other squares.

Designing and implementing this game makes a very good exercise in the use of graphics, and of linking two-dimensional variable arrays with one-dimensional control arrays. I'm afraid you will not produce a finished product that can rival the official version, as Visual Basic simply cannot deliver the same speed.

13.4 Graphics and control arrays

Two control arrays are used in the game – one to store a set of images that are wanted at points in the program, the second to form the visible playing surface. The latter one is mapped by two 2-D variable arrays that store the position of mines, and a count of the mines around each square.

The first job is to create a set of graphics for the blank tile, the mine, the flag, the explosion and the numbers. The second job to get them into controls on the form. Possible graphic designs and form layout are illustrated here.

Note that only 2 *imgBox* Images are placed on the form – just enough to start the control array. With a 10 × 10 grid of them, it would be extremely tedious and time-consuming to place them all by hand, especially as accurate positioning is essential. Fortunately, it is not necessary, thanks to the **Load** method.

```
Load imgBox(z)
```

This creates a new member for the *imgBox()* control array. It does not copy any of the Properties from the existing members. These must all be set after Loading, but run through a Loop, it doesn't take much code. You can see this in the **Form_Load** procedure, in particular the way that the Top and Left values are calculated.

```
imgBox(z).Top = y
imgBox(z).Left = x
imgBox(z).Height = 480
imgBox(z).Width = 480
imgBox(z).Visible = True
z = z + 1
x = x + 480
If x > 4320 Then
    x = 0
    y = y - 480
End If
```

My *imgBox* images happen to be 480 Twips square. If yours are anything different, make the x and y adjustments match the Width and Height of your Boxes. When the x values is more than 9 times the image width, it is time to start a new line – resetting x to 0 and moving y up by the height of the image.

The pictures are not copied into the *imgBox* controls at that point. This is done in the *initialise* procedure which is run at the start of each new game. Notice that instead of automatically loading a blank into every box, the code tests to see whether it is already blank. This helps to speed up the process. Copying a graphic from an existing control is far quicker than loading it from file, but still takes an appreciable time, and if you don't need to do it, then so much the better.

```
For z = 0 To 99
    If box(z) <> imgBlamk Then imgBox(z) = imgBlank
Next z
```

13.5 1-D and 2-D arrays

It is an unfortunate fact of Visual Basic that control arrays can only have one dimension, as this makes for extra work when you try to use them in conjunction with two-dimensional variable arrays. The correspondence between the 1-D and 2-D arrays is illustrated in Figure 13.4.

	0	1	2	3	4	5	6	7	8	9
9	90	91	92	93	94	95	96	97	98	99
8	80	81	82	83	84	85	86	87	88	89
...										
1	10	11	12	13	14	15	16	17	18	19
0	0	1	2	3	4	5	6	7	8	9

Figure 13.4 How the the 1-D control array fits into the 2-D variable arrays.

To convert from a control array index to the x, y values of a 2-D array you need formulae of the type:

```
x = Index \ 10
y = Index Mod 10
```

Thus an Index of 12 splits into:

```
x = 12 \ 10 = 1
y = 12 Mod 10 = 2
```

If we were simply using a variable array to store the positions of the mines, we could have used a one-dimensional array for this (the fact that the board appears two-dimensional on screen being irrelevant to the system), but we are also using an array to store the numbers of mines around each square. The shot of the game given opposite shows the relation of the numbers to the mines. Those calculations are much easier to do in 2-D.

Let's look a little closer at this. At an early stage in the *initialise* procedure, the *boxes()* array is filled with '0's to clear it of old mines, then 20 new ones are scattered through it at random by marking elements with a '1'. To find the number of mines adjacent to any square, we add up the '1's and '0's in the neighbouring *boxes()* elements. This could be done as a square is cleared, but it is more efficient to scan the whole board at the start of the game and store the results in an array.

The routine is a little dense as it needs 4 nested loops – the outer two to work through the board row by column, and the inner two to scan around each square – and we must avoid stepping off the board when scanning edge squares.

The game has just come to a sticky end. There were two possibilities in the bottom left corner – the mines could also have been beneath the 2 and 3. I guessed wrong.

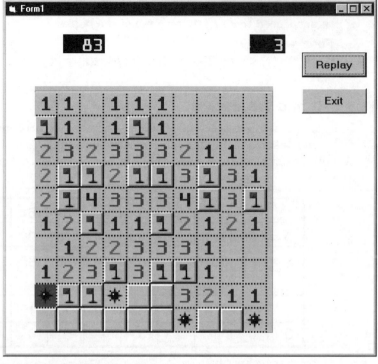

Figure 13.5 Minesweeper in action.

Using the board in the screenshot, work through the routine for a few of the squares – include at least one edge square in your dry run to see how it copes with edges.

```
For x = 0 To 9
    For y = 0 To 9
        num(x, y) = 0
        For y1 = y - 1 To y + 1
            For x1 = x - 1 To x + 1
                If y1 >= 0 And y1 < 10 Then
                    If x1 >= 0 And x1 < 10 Then num(x, y) = num(x, y) + boxes(x1, y1)
                End If
            Next x1
        Next y1
    Next y
Next x
```

We will tackle the rest of the design problems as we work through the code.

13.6 Game design and coding

Variables

Apart from the two arrays, we also need variables to count the number of flags placed (*found*) and mines cleared (*cleared*).

You could equally well store the values in Labels if you wanted a running display of progress. If you do this, name the Labels *found* and *cleared* (forget the lbl convention for once!) to match the code.

general declarations

Dim boxes(9, 9) As Integer	' 1 = mine 0 = clear
Dim num(9, 9) As Integer	' number of nearby mines
Dim found As Integer	' mines flagged
Dim cleared As Integer	' squares cleared

Setting up and initialising the game

This has been largely explained in Section 5. The **Load** procedure simply creates the imgBoxes to set up the board. Note that the initial x and y values and the adjustments should be tailored to the size and position of your first two *imgBox* Images.

```
Private Sub Form_Load()
    Randomize
    z = 2
    x = 960
    y = 4440
    Do
        Load imgBox(z)
        imgBox(z).Top = y
        imgBox(z).Left = x
        imgBox(z).Height = 480
        imgBox(z).Width = 480
        imgBox(z).Visible = True

        z = z + 1
        x = x + 480
        If x > 4320 Then
            x = 0
            y = y - 480
        End If
    Loop Until z = 100
    initialise
End Sub
```

Tip: If you omit the Randomize statement at first, the mines will always be placed under the same squares. This could be useful when testing and debugging the program. Remember to put it back before you ask anyone else to have a go!

The **initialise()** resets the variables and the arrays – remember that this is called before a new game, as well as at the very start of the program.

Notice in the random-placing routine that there is a check to make sure that you do not get two mines in the same square.

With 20 mines and 100 squares, the likelihood of double-booking is quite high. If you want to give your game different levels of difficulty, a first step would be to ask the players how many mines they would like.

```
Sub initialise ()
    Dim x As Integer, y As Integer, z As Integer
    Dim x1 As Integer, y1 As Integer
    found = 0                           ' reset all counts
    cleared = 0
    lblMinesLeft.Caption = 20
    lblClock.Caption = 0

' Blank box array
    For z = 0 To 99
        If imgBox(z) <> imgBlank Then imgBox(z) = imgBlank
    Next z

' zero boxes and check arrays
    For x = 0 To 9
        For y = 0 To 9
            boxes(x, y) = 0
        Next y
    Next x
' generate 20 random mines
    n = 0
    Do
        r = Int(Rnd(1) * 90)
        x = r \ 10
        y = r Mod 10
        If boxes(x, y) = 0 Then
            boxes(x, y) = 1
            n = n + 1
        End If
    Loop Until n = 20

' calculate number of mines near each square
    For x = 0 To 9
        For y = 0 To 9
            num(x, y) = 0
            For y1 = y - 1 To y + 1
                For x1 = x - 1 To x + 1
                    If y1 >= 0 And y1 < 10 Then
                        If x1 >= 0 And x1 < 10 Then num(x, y) = num(x, y) +
                            boxes(x1, y1)              ' all one line
                    End If
                Next x1
            Next y1
        Next y
    Next x
    timer1.Enabled = True              ' start the clock
End Sub
```

13.7 Mouse actions

The player's clicks are picked up by the **MouseDown** event on the *imgBox* control array. This procedure picks up five values from the system:

Private Sub imgBox_MouseDown(index As Integer, Button As Integer, Shift As Integer, x As Single, y As Single)

We are interested in the first two – the *index* number of the *imgBox*, the identifying number of the *button* (1 = Left, 2 = Right).

The procedure has four distinct parts.

1. Convert the Index to x, y values.
2. If the right button is down and the square is not flagged,
     give the square a flag graphic
     add one to the found count and display.
3. If the left button is down and the square is either flagged or untouched
     if there is a mine underneath,
       end the game with a bang
     if not, clear the box.
4. If all mines are found and all other squares cleared
     end the game successfully.

Notice that we can check the state of the *imgBox* control by comparing it to the *imgFlag* and other graphics stored in Images. As Picture is the main value for an Image, we do not need to specify this property when checking or assigning values.

```
If button = 2 And imgBox(index) <> imgFlag Then
    imgBox(index) = imgFlag
```

The box-clearing and losing game-end routines are fairly complex. Splitting them off into separate procedures makes the program significantly easier to develop and to read later.

```
Private Sub imgBox_mousedown (index As Integer, button As Integer, Shift As Integer, x As Single, y As Single)
    Dim x1 As Integer, y1 As Integer
    x1 = index \ 10
    y1 = index Mod 10
    ' right button and box not flagged
    If button = 2 And imgBox(index) <> imgFlag Then
        imgBox(index) = imgFlag
        found = found + 1
        lblMinesLeft.Caption = Val(lblMinesLeft.Caption) - 1
    Else
    ' left button and imgBox not cleared
    If button = 1 And (imgBox(index) = imgBlank Or imgBox(index) = imgFlag) Then
        If boxes(x1, y1) = 1 Then gameover (index)
        Else Call clearbox(x1, y1)
        End If
    End If

    If cleared + found = 100 Then          ' all found?
        MsgBox "Success"
```

```
            timer1.Enabled = False
        End If
    End Sub
```

The *clearbox* subroutine should lift up the tile to display the number of nearby mines, and if this is zero, spread out from there to clear the adjacent squares, carrying on recursively until we have a blank area with a fringe of numbered squares. It should do, but I gave up after doing the adjacent squares. If you would like to take the time to make the routine recursive, you're welcome. Note the use of the *reveal* procedure to save duplication.

```
    Sub clearbox (x As Integer, y As Integer)
        Dim x1 As Integer, y1 As Integer
        Call reveal(x, y)
        ' if clear, reveal all around
        If num(x, y) = 0 Then
            For y1 = y - 1 To y + 1
                For x1 = x - 1 To x + 1
                    If y1 >= 0 And y1 < 10 Then
                        If x1 >= 0 And x1 < 10 Then Call reveal(x1, y1)
                    End If
                Next x1
            Next y1
        End If
    End Sub
```

The *reveal* subroutine shouldn't have to do much more than display the underlying number and add to the *cleared* count, but we must allow players to clear a square that had previously been flagged. To do this, we must reset the *found* count and the display. When displaying the number of surrounding mines, *num(x,y)* gives us the number, which is used as the index for the *NumPic()* array to get the graphic.

```
    Sub reveal (ByVal x As Integer, ByVal y As Integer)
        index = x * 10 + y
        ' if flagged reset mines count
        If imgBox(index) = imgFlag Then
            lblMinesLeft.Caption = Val(lblMinesLeft.Caption) + 1
            found = found - 1
            cleared = cleared + 1
        End If
        If imgBox(index) = imgBlank Then cleared = cleared + 1
        imgBox(index) = imgNum(num(x, y))
    End Sub
```

The losing end game explodes the mine, then scans the box array for any unflagged mines and displays them. The Index value that is passed to here is the one picked up by the **imgBox_MouseDown** procedure.

```
    Sub gameover (index As Integer)
        Dim x As Integer, y As Integer, z As Integer
        timer1.Enabled = False                          ' stop the clock
        imgBox(index) = imgBang                         ' explode the mine
```

```
    For z = 0 To 99                          ' display remaining mines
        If z <> index Then
            x = z \ 10
            y = z Mod 10
            If imgBox(z) = imgBlank And boxes(x, y) = 1 Then ' unflagged mine
                imgBox(z) = imgMine
            End If
        End If
    Next z
End Sub
```

The rest of the code is obvious. The *Replay* button simply calls up initialise to restart the game; *Quit* is the usual End; and the *Timer* runs the clock. Its interval should be set to 1000 at design time.

```
Sub cmdReplay_Click ()
    initialise
End Sub

Sub cmdQuit_Click ()
    End
End Sub

Sub Timer1_Timer ()
    lblClock.Caption = Val(lblClock.Caption) + 1
End Sub
```

13.8 Exercises

1. Make a Visual Basic 'flick-book' by creating a set of pictures displaying some kind of activity – a matchstick person doing aerobics, a machine in motion with flashing lights and whirling wheels, the cow jumping over the moon, or whatever. They should all be the same size (the smaller they are, the faster they can be manipulated), and stored in an Image array. Use a Timer to cycle through them on screen, changing images 10 times a second or faster, looping back to the start after the last in the set has been displayed.

2. Write a Hangman game, with appropriate graphics. The scaffold can be erected by having a set of graphics, covering the stages of construction, and displaying the next in the sequence each time a wrong letter is guessed.

3. New Windows users need training in the use of the mouse. Write a program to run a game that will give them practice in positioning the mouse accurately. It should display small images briefly at random places on the screen. The user must click on them before they disappear to score points. Varying levels of difficulty can be created by reducing the time that the images are displayed; placing two or more on screen simultaneously; having four types of images – those to be clicked with the left button, those to be clicked with the right, those to be double-clicked, and those which must *not* be clicked at all.

Possible solutions for these Exercises are included in the Lecturer's Supplement disk.

The files for the *Minesweeper* program are available from the Visual Basic page at the author's Web site: http://www.tcp.co.uk/~macbride

14 MDI Forms

With the use of MDI forms, you can create applications that have windows within windows.

14.1 MDI – Parent and Child

A common feature of Windows applications is to have windows within the main window of the program. In Visual Basic, this is achieved through MDI – Multiple Document Interface – Forms. If a project contains an MDI form, then any ordinary forms which have their *MDIChild* property set to True will appear as windows within it, at runtime. Other forms, that are not designated as children, appear as normal.

As MDI forms are only intended for use as containers for other forms, there are limitations on the controls that can be placed on them.

- They can have menus, though as these will be replaced by the menus on the Child form, they would normally carry only a small set of commands to open Child forms and exit the program.

- They can also take Picture box controls, and other types of controls can be placed within a Picture box. The underlying idea here is that the Picture box will form a ToolBar, with Images displaying icons for the tools.

Child forms are designed and used largely as normal. At design time, the form is handled as a separate entity, but keep its runtime size and position in mind when laying out controls. When the program is executed, the form will be shrunk to fit within the MDI form. During the running of the program, if you offer Cascade and Tile options to allow your users to tidy up their display, then the shape of the inner forms will change again. Perhaps the most important thing to remember when designing these forms is to set their MDIChild property to True!

As a general rule, you would only set up one Child form at design time, and create additional forms as needed during runtime, either by using an array of forms or by Loading new instances of the original form. The array approach is used in the example given below. The program acts as a gallery to display bitmapped graphics. It has a *painting* array (of forms) which is linked to the visible *frmPaint* forms, by making the *Tag* property of the Form equal to the index of the array.

14.2 The gallery

To create this program, you will need an MDI Form, named *frmMDIGallery,* a Child Form, named *frmPaint*, the File Selector form that we have used previously, plus one basic module, here called *painting.bas*. Apart from the File Selector, the forms in this demonstration carry no controls except for menus. When you have got it working, you may like to add a ToolBar, made up from a Picture box and a set of Images, to the MDI form, with the Click events on the images calling up the menu options. If you prefer, you could add an Image to the Child form and load pictures into there rather than directly onto the form. This would allow you to fit borders around the graphics, and use the (coloured) background of the form as a frame.

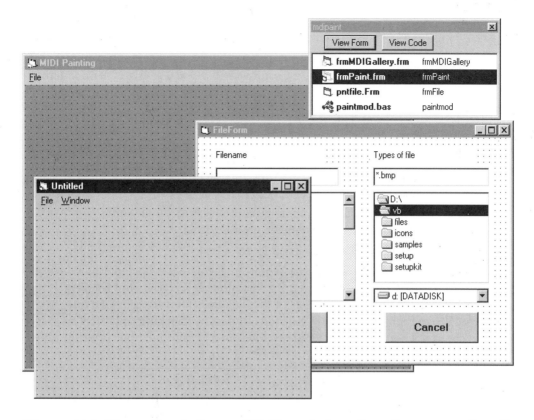

Figure 14.1 The gallery's forms. FileForm is based on the one used earlier.

The menus

There are menus in both the Parent and the Child forms:

frmMDIGallery		frmPaint	
File		File	Window
Open		Open	Cascade
Exit		Close	Tile
		Exit	Arrange Icons

The activities of this program have been kept to an absolute minimum so that we can focus on the manipulation of the forms – Open, Close and Window management. If you want the Window menu to display a list of the open Child Form windows, so that your user can switch between them by clicking on their names, set the *mnuWindow* object's *WindowList* property to True.

Global variables

These should be declared in the basic module before turning to the code on the forms.

```
Global painting() As New frmPaint
Global blank()
Global fname As String          ' for use with the File Selector form
Global FileIO As Boolean
Global PaintNum As Integer      ' count of elements in the array
```

In *painting* we have an array of forms, all of which will share the properties of *frmPaint*. *blank()* has not been typed, but could be Integer. The elements in there will be set to True when the related element of *painting()* has been closed and is therefore available for reuse. Initially, the *blank()* values will all be 0 – False. Neither array has been given a fixed dimension. Their sizes will be changed with **ReDim** during the run, each time a new form is opened.

The MDI Form and its code

You cannot turn an ordinary form into a MDI form, as they have their own special Properties. The first job is therefore to create the form! Open the **Insert** menu and select **MDI Form**.

The form itself is blank, and its Properties can be left at the default – though you may like to set the colours and a Caption.

Use the Menu Editor to set up the File menu.

Very little code is needed on this form. When the form is first loaded, the *painting* and *blank* arrays are ReDimmed and their initial values set. Notice that the **Tag** property of *painting(1)* is set to 1. The purpose of the Tag is to identify the form and link it to the array. When there are several Child forms open, by checking the Tag of the current one, we can tell where it fits in the array. Look out for similar lines later, linking the Tag number to the array element.

```
Private Sub MDIForm_Load ()
    Show
    ReDim painting(1)
    ReDim blank(1)
    painting(1).Tag = 1
    painting(1).Show
    blank(1) = True
    PaintNum = 1
End Sub
```

The *Open* menu option in the MDI form serves the same purpose as the *Open* option on the Child window. Rather than duplicate code, it has been written into a procedure, *FileOpen*, and stored on the basic module so that it is available to all forms.

```
Private Sub mnuOpen_Click ()
    FileOpen
End Sub
Private Sub mnuQuit_Click ()
    End
End Sub
```

The Paintfrm code

This is an ordinary form, but you must set its **MDIChild** property to *True*. Again, there are no controls on this form, unless you want to display the pictures in an Image control. (Though this is a refinement you would be advised to leave until you have the simple system running.) During runtime, the forms' captions are the filenames of the displayed graphics.

You may notice here that some menu options have the same control names as those on the MDI form. This does not cause any conflict as they are on different forms. *Open* and *Quit* are also exactly the same as those on the MDI. The *Close* calls up the form's **Unload** method to remove the form from the MDI window and mark the empty array.

```
Private Sub mnuOpen_Click ()
    FileOpen
End Sub

Private Sub mnuQuit_Click ()
    End
End Sub

Private Sub mnuClose_Click ()
    Unload Me
End Sub

Private Sub Form_Unload (Cancel As Integer)
    blank(Me.Tag) = True
End Sub
```

Me refers to the current form. Used in the **mnuClose** procedure, it tells the system which form to Unload. Used in the **Unload** procedure, its *Tag* property gives the index of the corresponding element in the array.

The *Window* options use the **Arrange** method on the MDI form to reorganise the display. The method has four options:

0 = Cascade

1 = Tile, splitting the screen horizontally at first

2 = Tile, splitting the screen vertically at first

3 = Arrange icons

With both of the **Tile** options, the screen is divided horizontally *and* vertically once you have more than three windows.

```
Private Sub mnuArrange_Click ()
    frmMDIGallery.Arrange 3        'Icon arrange mode
End Sub

Private Sub mnuCascade_Click ()
    frmMDIGallery.Arrange 0        'Cascade mode
End Sub

Private Sub mnuTile_Click ()
    frmMDIGallery.Arrange  2       'Vertical Tile mode
End Sub
```

14.3 Opening files and forms

The trickiest aspect of this program is co-ordinating the array of forms. You want your users to be able to have as many forms open as they like, and to be able to close down any one of them at any time. If you simply extend the array to create a new form each time another graphic is opened, and Unload forms when one is closed, you could finish up with a large, but largely empty, array. This is an unnecessary waste of space – and we are storing forms here, not simple numbers, so the space used is significant. We

One of the limitations of slapping graphics directly onto a form, rather than in an Image, is that they always tuck themselves into the top left corner and if their backgrounds are the same colour as the form, there is no way to see where they end. Using an image is a little more bother, but worth the effort.

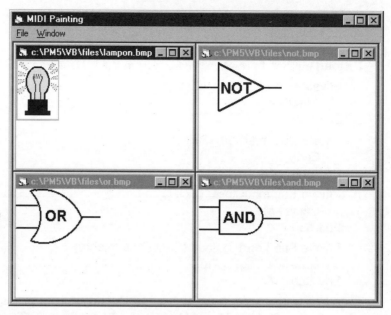

Figure 14.2 The gallery in use.

can make better use of memory if we keep a track of array elements that are no longer active and reuse them when opening forms, only extending the array if there are no empty slots in the array.

The design for the file/form opening routine can be summarised:

    1. Get filename from File Selector – abandoning if no suitable name produced
        pass control to the File form and wait for its feedback
    2. Find an empty space in the array or make a new one at the end
        2.1 Loop through the empty array
            2.1.1 if a True value is found
                use the element number as the index number
                set the element to False
                jump out of the routine
            2.1.2 if there are no spaces
                add another element to painting and blank
                and use PaintNum as the index
    3. Set up the new form's Tag, Caption and Picture, and Show it.

This all could be done in one procedure, but the code is made more readable by slicing off the empty space finding routine into a separate function, here called *GetIndex*.

Using the File Selector form

The *FileOpen* procedure uses the File Selector form in a different way from previously. In earlier programs, this form had served two purposes – collecting filenames for both opening and saving. This time, we only want to open files. The *FileIO* variable is here defined as a Boolean, and will be True if a suitable file is found.

The focus is passed to the File form, then the routine goes into a loop, containing the single statement:

    DoEvents

It stays there, awaiting input from the user, until a filename has been set or the Open routine cancelled.

```
Sub FileOpen()
    fname = ""
    FileIO = True
    frmFile.Show
    frmFile.SetFocus
    Do
        DoEvents
    Loop Until fname <> "" Or Not FileIO        ' OK or Cancel on the File form
    If fname = "" Or Not FileIO Then Exit Sub
    If UCase(Right(fname, 4)) <> ".BMP" Then Exit Sub
    findex = GetIndex()
    painting(findex).Tag = findex               ' links Tag to array index
    painting(findex).Caption = fname
    painting(findex).Picture = LoadPicture(fname)
    painting(findex).Show
End Sub
```

The code on the OK and Cancel buttons of the File form is very simple. OK gives the filename; Cancel sets the FileIO variable to False. Both then hide the File form.

```
Private Sub cmdOK_Click()
    fname = File1.Path & "\" & txtFilename
    frmFile.Hide
End Sub

Private Sub cmdCancel_Click()
    FileIO = False
    frmFile.Hide
End Sub
```

Opening the file is only the first step. We then have to create a new form in the array and set it up with its picture. Creating the form is handled through the *GetIndex* functions. There are two points to note here.

1. There are two possible ways of getting a suitable index value, so there are two possible exits – an *Exit Function* line within the *For ... Next* loop, and the normal *End*.

2. When the arrays are redimensioned, the **Preserve** option is used in the **ReDim** line. Without this, the existing data in the arrays would be cleared out and the arrays set up afresh.

```
Function GetIndex() As Integer
    Dim element As Integer
    For element = 1 To paintnum
        If blank(element) Then
            GetIndex = element
            blank(element) = False
            Exit Function
        End If
    Next element
```

```
            paintnum = paintnum + 1
            ReDim Preserve painting(paintnum)
            ReDim Preserve blank(paintnum)
            GetIndex = paintnum
        End Function
```

14.4 Exercises

1. Extend the program developed in this chapter so that it will display notes in a Text Box beneath the painting, which must now be held in an Image.

Hint: To keep the picture and its notes together, write the picture's filename into the note text, which is then saved as a file. It is this file that the user will select. When the file is opened, the picture filename can be read from it, and used to open its file.

---

2. Add an MDI form to the electronic diary program that was set as an exercise at the end of Chapter 12, and adapt the program so that several 'pages' can be displayed at once on individual Child forms.

3. Adapt the Text Editor program (again), adding an MDI form to it, so that several text files can be viewed and edited at the same time.

   Possible solutions for Exercises 2 and 3 are included in the Lecturer's Supplement disk.

15 The Common Dialog control

This is a multi-purpose control for interacting with the Windows system. Just place one Common Dialog control on a form, and you can have standard Windows Save, Open, Print, Font, Color and Help dialog boxes in your program.

The type of dialog box cannot be defined at design time, but is set at the appropriate point in the code by one of these methods: **ShowOpen**, **ShowSave**, **ShowPrint**, **ShowFont**, **ShowColor** and **ShowHelp**.

The properties of a Common Dialog box *can* be set at design time, though as most properties are only relevant to certain types of dialog box, it makes sense to set them just before the box is brought into play.

15.1 Adding the Common Dialog control

If you cannot see this control  in your Toolbox, add it now.

- Open the Tools menu and select Custom Controls.
- Scroll down through the list of options until you find Microsoft Common Dialog control, and click on it to place a cross in the checkbox.

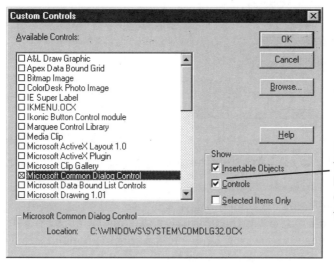

If you cannot see it in the Available Controls list, make sure that Controls is checked in the Show frame.

Add the control in the normal way, placing it in any convenient spot – it will be invisible at runtime, and the position of the (visible) dialog boxes is determined by the system, not by anything that you can do.

15.2 Worked example

The best way to understand how the Common Dialog control works is to see it in action, in its various guises. Almost all of these have special properties that must be set before they can be used safely.

The example program is a simple NotePad, with routines to let you save, open and print text files, and to set the font and colours of the Text Box. All of these use the Common Dialog control, and all are run from buttons. You can see, on the layout, that there is one for each Show... method – and two for ShowColor, so that both the ForeColor and BackColor can be changed.

I have named the Common Dialog control *CD1*. The name will have to be typed many times in this program, so the shorter the better!

In the example, the Text Box, *txtPad*, has had its **MultiLine** property set to *True*, and its **ScrollBars** property set to *Vertical,* so that the text wraps round when it meets the edge of the box. These settings are optional.

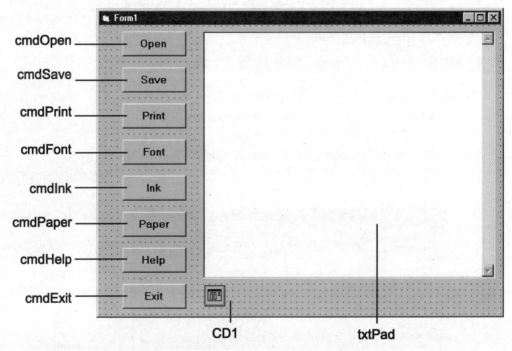

Figure 15.1 The layout for the Common Dialog demo program.

15.3 Error-trapping

In any version of the Common Dialog box, if the user clicks **Cancel**, the system generates an error. This will crash the program if it is not trapped. You do not need to do anything in response to the error – if the user wants to abandon a routine, that's not a problem and will not affect anything else. You will find that all procedures open with the line:

    On Error GoTo cancelled

and have the target at the exit.

    cancelled:
    End Sub

If you also wanted to pick up and respond to errors caused by missing files or printer problems, you would have to check the error codes and respond appropriately. The focus here is on the Common Dialog control, so let's keep error-trapping to a minimum.

15.4 Program code

Open

The **ShowOpen** method produces an **Open** file dialog box. This does not actually open a file – it simply gets the name of a file, which can then be opened within the code.

Set the Filter property
to define the types

The default is to open as Readonly, so the file cannot be saved
again with the same name.

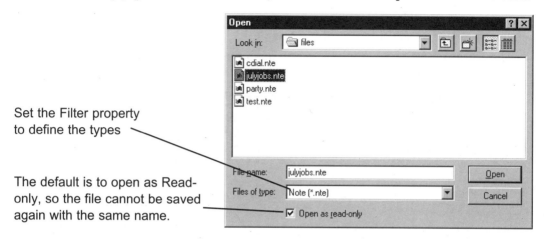

Figure 15.2 The Open file dialog box.

If you want to restrict the display to certain file types, you can set the **Filter** property. The definition is a string expression with two parts – the first is the text to be shown in the **Files of type** slot; the second is the file specification. In this case, the statement:

CD1.Filter = "Note (*.nte)| *.nte"

sets up the dialog box so that it will only display files with an extension of *.nte*, which is being used to identify files produced by this program.

You can also to set the initial directory with the **InitDir** property, e.g.,

CD1.InitDir = "C:\vb"

The Open dialog box returns the selected filename in the **FileName** property. This should be copied to a simple variable. The file can then be opened with the normal **Open...** statement.

Here's the full code for the **Open** button.

```
Private Sub cmdOpen_Click()
    On Error GoTo cancelled
    CD1.Filter = "Note (*.nte)| *.nte"
    CD1.ShowOpen
    filename = CD1.filename
    If filename = "" Then Exit Sub
    Open filename For Input As #1
     Input #1, temp
    txtPad.Text = temp
    Close #1
    cancelled:
End Sub
```

Save

The **ShowSave** method opens the **Save As** dialog box. As with the **Open** version, you should set the **Filter** and **InitDir** first, if required, and take the name of the file from the **FileName** property afterwards.

You may also wish to set up the **FileName** at the start. It could be given the name of the current file, if one has been opened, or given a default name such as *Untitled1*, or simply cleared – the choice in this example.

The **DefaultExt** property is also worth defining. This specifies the extension to tack onto the name, if the user does not type one.

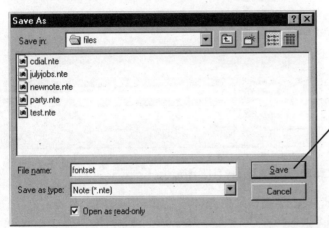

Don't let the Save button fool you. This just returns control to the program code – it's up to you to collect the filename and save the file.

Figure 15.3 The Save file dialog box.

The code follows the same pattern as that on the Open button.

```
Private Sub cmdSave_Click()
    On Error GoTo cancelled
    CD1.filename = ""
    CD1.Filter = "Note (*.nte)| *.nte"
    CD1.DefaultExt = "nte"
    CD1.ShowSave
    filename = CD1.filename
    If filename ="" Then Exit Sub
    Open filename For Output As #1
    temp = txtPad.Text
    Write #1, temp
    Close #1
    cancelled:
End Sub
```

Print

ShowPrinter opens the Print dialog box and, as before, this is just a means of setting options – you still need to write code to do the actual printing.

Reading and dealing with the options raises some problems. The number of copies is easy enough – that value is returned through the **Copies** property, and a **For ... Next** loop will print the number required.

Your Print dialog box will look different, unless you also happen to be using a Brother laser printer!

In the Print Range frame, the All and Selection options will be active, but probably not Pages.

You can use the Copies property to set the default number of copies or find out how many have been requested.

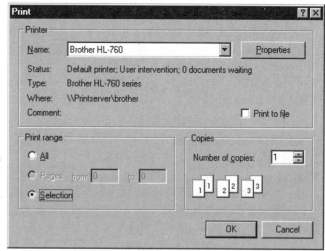

Figure 15.4 The Print dialog box.

To find out which Print Range has been selected, you have to explore the **Flags** property. Flags holds several different settings, each indicated by the state of a particular bit in the property – 1 usually meaning On and 0 meaning Off.

We can tell if the user has chosen to print **All** the text or a **Selection**, by examining the very last bit of the value. And the easiest way to do this is with a Mod 2 division. If the remainder is 1, it shows that last bit is set, meaning that Selection has been chosen. If the remainder is 0, All has been chosen.

Note: The Mod 2 trick only works where you want to know the state of the last bit. If you want to set or get the values of other bits, you will have to use the AND and OR bitwise operators. There is no room to go into those in this slim book.

We send **txtPad.SelText** to the printer if Selection is chosen, and **txtPad.Text** if All is chosen. In both cases, **EndDoc** is needed to output the final page. Here's the code.

```
Private Sub cmdPrint_Click()
    On Error GoTo cancelled
    CD1.ShowPrinter
    For n = 1 To CD1.Copies
        If CD1.Flags = 1 Then   'Selection
            Printer.Print txtPad.SelText
            Printer.EndDoc
        Else
            If CD1.Flags = 0 Then 'all text
                Printer.Print txtPad.Text
                Printer.EndDoc
            End If
        End If
    Next n
    cancelled:
End Sub
```

Font

Before you can use ShowFont to open this dialog box, you must tell the system which types of fonts to include in the list. You can use printer fonts, screen fonts or both, and the setting is done through the **Flags** property. The easiest approach here is to use one of the built-in constants. **cdlCFBoth** selects both types of fonts – the value 3 would have the same effect, but **cdlCFBoth** may be more meaningful. The simple statement:

    CD1.Flags = cdlCFBoth

sets the font selection, though is also erases any other Flag settings. Fortunately, these don't seem to have any effect.

After the Font dialog box has been closed, your code must update the Font settings for the Text Box. There is no quick and easy way of doing this – each aspect of the font needs a separate line.

```
Private Sub cmdFont_Click()
    On Error GoTo cancelled
    CD1.FontName = txtPad.Font
    CD1.Flags = cdlCFBoth
    CD1.ShowFont
    txtPad.FontName = CD1.FontName
    txtPad.FontSize = CD1.FontSize
    txtPad.FontBold = CD1.FontBold
    txtPad.FontItalic = CD1.FontItalic
    txtPad.FontUnderline = CD1.FontUnderline
cancelled:
End Sub
```

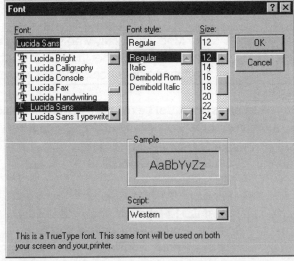

To list only screen fonts, set the Flags to 1 or **cdlCFScreenFonts**.

To list only printer fonts, set Flags to 2 or **cdlCFPrinterFonts**.

Figure 15.5 The Font dialog box.

Colours

The **ShowColor** method raises no problems – except for needing separate routines for the ForeColor and BackColor! The only relevant property is **Color**. You should set this to the current colour before you go into the dialog box, though that is not essential. Afterwards, just copy the colour to appropriate property of the object you are re-colouring – in this case, txtPad.

Here's the **Ink** (ForeColor) button's code:

```
Private Sub cmdInk_Click()
    On Error GoTo cancelled
    CD1.Color = txtPad.ForeColor
    CD1.ShowColor
    txtPad.ForeColor = CD1.Color
    cancelled:
End Sub
```

The **Paper** button's code is identical but with **BackColor** instead of **ForeColor**.

The default settings give you a box with the **Custom Colors** pane open. If you like to mess with the Flags, you can get the smaller **Basic colors** display.

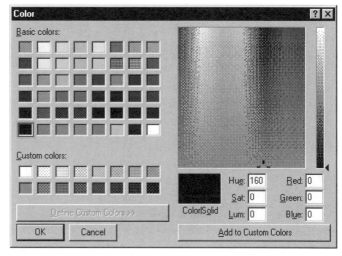

Figure 15.6 The Color dialog box.

Help

ShowHelp calls up the standard Help system, displaying a chosen Help file. For test purposes, use any convenient .HLP file that you have on your computer. If you want to use this in earnest, giving specific help on a program on your own, you will have to create your own Help file. Writing a Help file is beyond the scope of this book.

Before calling **ShowHelp**, you must set the **HelpCommand** property which determines how it starts. The most useful setting is to open at the Contents list. For this set the value to 3 or use the constant **cdlHelpContents**.

Here's the code – using the Visual Basic Help file.

```
Private Sub cmdHelp_Click()
    On Error GoTo cancelled
    CD1.HelpFile = "vb.HLP"
    CD1.HelpCommand = cdlHelpContents
    CD1.ShowHelp
    cancelled:
End Sub
```

Task 15.1 Find out how Windows Help files are created. Is any special software needed? A good place to do your research will be at Microsoft's site on the Internet. Its URL is http://www.microsoft.com

15.5 Exercises

1. Replace the File Selector form in the MDI Gallery program (Chapter 14) with a Common Dialog control, using the ShowOpen method.

2. Take the final version of the Text Editor (Chapter 10) and replace its Font and File routines with ones that use the Common Dialog control.

16 Data controls

As you were wading through the earlier chapters on sequential and random access files, you may have wondered whether there was an easier way of handling databases. Here's the good news – there is. The next example program can read, update and add new records to a relational database created in Microsoft Access, and the only code in the whole program is an **End** on the Quit button!

If you want to create a new database, you will have to write code, but the **Data** control and the related *data-aware* controls contain within themselves all the code that is needed to access and edit existing databases. It will take you a few moments and a little thought to set the properties to create the necessary links, but that's about all that is essential.

16.1 The controls

Some controls are *data-aware* – specifically designed for use with databases:

 The **Data** control creates a link to a table in a database, and allows you to move through the records in that table. When placed on a form, it can be closed up so that only the movement arrows are visible |◄| ◄ | ► | ►|, or opened out to show its Caption |◄| ◄ | Data1 ► | ►| .

 The **DBList** and 🔲 **DBCombo** controls can be used where you have two or more tables in the database, and a field in one draws its data from a related field in another.

Some normal controls can display field data. You can use:

- Text Boxes for fields that are open for editing;
- CheckBoxes and Option buttons for Yes/No or True/False values;
- Labels for data that the user should not edit;
- Images, PictureBoxes and OLE for bitmaps and other imported objects.

16.2 The database

Before you can start on the program, you must have a database. The one used here is a simple stock control database, created in Microsoft Access. It contains two tables.

Table1 has these fields:

Name	Type
ID	AutoNumber
Item	Text
Cost Price	Currency
SupplierRef	Lookup, drawing its options from Supplier in Table 2

Table2 has these fields:

Name	Type
Supplier	Text
Name	Text
TelNo	Text

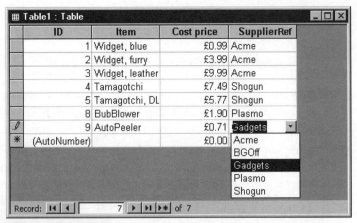

SupplierRef is a **Lookup** field, with its options drawn from the *Supplier* field in *Table2*. Your database should contain a similar field if you want to test out the data-aware controls

Figure 16.1 The stock database with some sample data.

16.3 The form

Place on the form two Data controls, at least two Text Boxes, for the simple text fields, one DBCombo control, for the Lookup field, and a Command Button. Please yourself about where the controls are placed, but do leave enough free space beneath the DBCombo for the drop-down list when the program is running. All the names can be left at the defaults. The properties can be set once the controls are all in place.

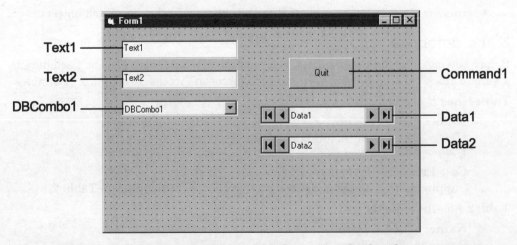

Figure 16.2 The controls needed for a simple database program.

Data1

If the database is from anywhere other than Access, go first to the **Connect** property and select the database type from the list.

Next, set the **DatabaseName**. Type this in if you know the exact path and filename, or click 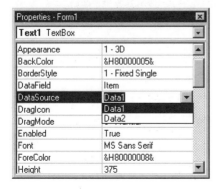 and browse through your folders to find it.

Complete the link to the data by setting the **RecordSource**. The system will check the selected database to find the names of its tables and display them in the drop-down list. Select the one you want.

If the program was for viewing, and not editing, a database, you would set **ReadOnly** to *True*. In this case, we want to be able to edit, so make sure that it is set to *False*.

If you want to let your users add new records, set **EOFAction** to *2 - AddNew*. This property defines what happens when the end of the file is reached.

Properties - Form1	
Data1 Data	
Align	0 - None
Appearance	1 - 3D
BackColor	&H80000005&
BOFAction	0 - Move First
Caption	Stock items
Connect	Access
DatabaseName	C:\My Documents\stock.mdb
DragIcon	(None)
DragMode	0 - Manual
Enabled	True
EOFAction	2 - Add New
Exclusive	False
Font	MS Sans Serif
ForeColor	&H80000008&
Height	375
Index	
Left	480
MouseIcon	(None)
MousePointer	0 - Default
Name	Data1
Negotiate	False
Options	0
ReadOnly	False
RecordsetType	1 - Dynaset
RecordSource	Table1
Tag	Table1
Top	Table2
Visible	True
WhatsThisHelpID	0
Width	2775

Data2

This should be set up in the same way as **Data1**, but setting the other table as the **RecordSource**.

Text1 and Text2

Setting up these and other simple controls, you just need to create a link to the appropriate field.

First select the **DataSource**. This will be the name of the Data control that is linked to the desired table.

Next select the **DataField**. The drop-down list should display the fields in the table.

Set the Font, Color and other Properties as normal.

Properties - Form1	
Text1 TextBox	
Appearance	1 - 3D
BackColor	&H80000005&
BorderStyle	1 - Fixed Single
DataField	Item
DataSource	Data1
DragIcon	Data1
DragMode	Data2
Enabled	True
Font	MS Sans Serif
ForeColor	&H80000008&
Height	375

Properties - Form1	
Text1 TextBox	
Appearance	1 - 3D
BackColor	&H80000005&
BorderStyle	1 - Fixed Single
DataField	Item
DataSource	ID
DragIcon	Item
DragMode	Cost price
	SupplierRef
Enabled	True
Font	MS Sans Serif
ForeColor	&H80000008&
Height	375

Figure 16.3 Select the DataSource and DataField from the drop-down lists.

DBCombo

This will produce a drop-down list, containing all the values in a field of one table, from which one can be selected as the data for the linked field in the other table. They are rather more complicated to set up, as you are having to make links between two tables and two fields.

The **DataSource** and **DataField** are defined as for simple controls, and identify the table (linked through a **Data** control) and the field which is to be displayed.

In this case, the **DataSource** is *Data1*, and the **DataField** is *SupplierRef*.

The **RowSource** is the **Data** control that is linked to table from which the values will be drawn – *Data2* which links to *Table2* (the suppliers' names and telephone numbers).

The **BoundColumn** is the field which contains the source data – *Supplier*.

The **ListField**, which determines the data to be listed, should also be set to the same field.

DBList controls are set up in the same way.

Properties - Form1	
DBCombo1 DBCombo	
Appearance	1 - 3D
BackColor	&H00FFFFFF&
BoundColumn	Supplier
DataField	SupplierRef
DataSource	Data1
DragIcon	(None)
DragMode	0 - Manual
Enabled	True
Font	MS Sans Serif
ForeColor	&H00000000&
Height	315
HelpContextID	0
Index	
IntegralHeight	True
Left	360
ListField	Supplier
Locked	False
MatchEntry	0 - Basic Matching
MouseIcon	(None)
MousePointer	0 - Default
Name	DBCombo1
RowSource	Data2
Style	Data1
TabIndex	Data2

16.4 Program code

Write an **End** statement in the Quit button. That's it!

When running the program, use the arrows to move between the records. Any changes that you make to a record will be stored when you move off it, or when the program ends. If you want to add a new record, go to the end of the file, then click the **Next** arrow to create a new, blank record.

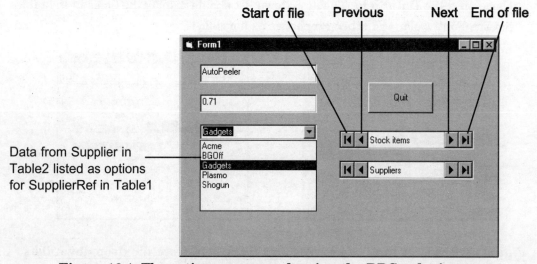

Data from Supplier in Table2 listed as options for SupplierRef in Table1

Figure 16.4 The active program, showing the DBCombo in use.

16.5 Improving the display

The appearance of any form, whether you are using Data controls or not, can be improved with a little thought and effort.

- For a more interesting background, set a large and relatively plain image as the **Picture** property of the form.

- If the data is to be entered into any Text Box, or other control, it should be accompanied by an identifying Label. Where there is a background Picture, the **BackStyle** of the Labels should be set to *Transparent*.

- You can make the Data control display the ID, or any other field of the current record by taking these steps:

   Add a Label, setting its **DataSource** as the control, and its **DataField** as the ID (and set **Visible** to *False*). In its Change procedure, write a line like this:

   Data1.Caption = " Record No. " & Label1

- If a Data control is present simply to provide a link to a table, and is not going to be used for moving between records, set its **Visible** property to *False*.

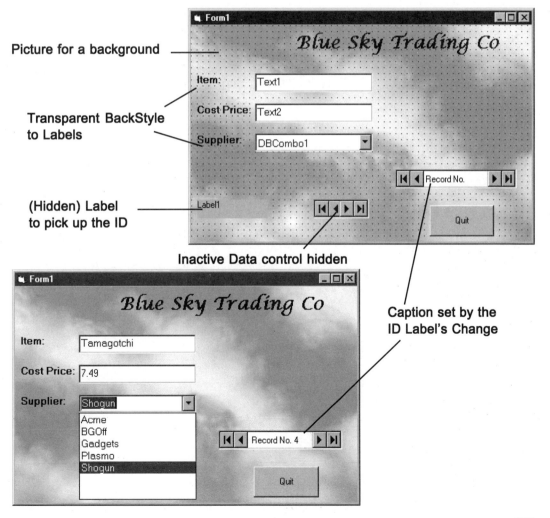

Picture for a background

Transparent BackStyle to Labels

(Hidden) Label to pick up the ID

Inactive Data control hidden

Caption set by the ID Label's Change

Appendix A: Solutions to exercises

Chapter 2

Exercise 1

The form should look something like this, though the layout and size of the controls are entirely up to you.

The code attached to the command button should read:

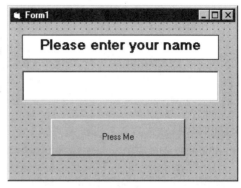

```
Private Sub Command1_Click ()
    Label1.Caption = Text1.Text
End Sub
```

Exercise 4

Here the Label has been given a caption using the Properties window, though this will be overwritten once the first button is clicked.

The code on the "Stop" button should read:

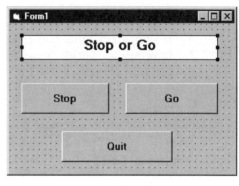

```
Private Sub Command1_Click ()
    Label1.Caption = "Stop"
    Label1.ForeColor = &HFF&
End Sub
```

That on the "Go" button should read:

```
Private Sub Command2_Click ()
    Label1.Caption = "Go"
    Label1.ForeColor = &HFF00&
End Sub
```

Your command button numbers may well be different. It depends entirely on the order in which they are added.

Chapter 3

Exercise 1

Your form should have two Text Boxes named *txtCelsius* and *txtFahrenheit*, (or *txtC* and *txtF* would do just as well, and save typing), and two buttons. The identifying Labels are purely decorative but worth adding. If you run the convert code from the Change event of *txtCelsius*, it should read:

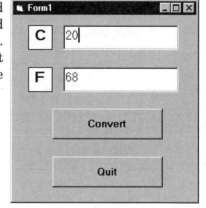

```
Private Sub Celsius_Change ()
txtFahrenheit = txtCelsius * 9 / 5 + 32
End Sub
```

Exercise 4

Edit the Convert button to read "Convert to F" and add another captioned "Convert to C". Their code should read:

```
Private Sub ConvToF_Change ()
    txtFahrenheit = txtCelsius * 9 / 5 + 32
End Sub
Private Sub ConvToC_Change ()
    txtCelsius = (Fahrenheit -32) * 5 / 9
End Sub
```

Chapter 4

Exercise 1

As only one statement is conditional on each test, these can be written as single-line Ifs. The over 50,000 and below 20,000 tests are simple, but to spot the middle range you must test both limits, linking the two expressions with an AND.

```
Private Sub Form_Click ()
    Dim salary As Single

    salary = InputBox("How much do you want to earn?")
    If salary > 50000 Then MsgBox "Don't go into writing"
    If salary > 20000 And salary <= 50000 Then MsgBox "Good luck"
    If salary <= 20000 Then MsgBox "What modest aims!"
End Sub
```

Exercise 2

The first trick to this is to note that if you end a Print line with a semi-colon, it does not move the print position down to the start of the next line. For example:

```
For n = 1 To 10              For n = 1 To 10
    print "*";   'semicolon      print "*"
Next n                       Next n
```

The code on the left will produce a line of asterisks across the screen, that on the right, will produce a line down the screen.

The second trick is to make use of the fact that the end value in a **For ... Next** loop can be a variable. This gives us a link between the outer and inner loops.

```
Private Sub Form_Click ()
    For outer = 8 To 1 Step -1
        Print outer;
        For inner = 1 To outer
            Print "*";
        Next inner
        Print
    Next outer
End Sub
```

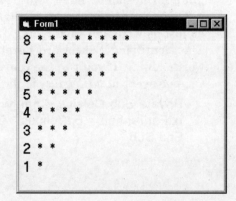

Exercise 3

The solution shown here has much room for improvement, but it works. The user types the Table number into *txtTable*. The random number is generated by code on *cmdProblem*, and stored in *lblMult*. *cmdCheck* tests the value in *txtAnswer* against *txtTable * lblMult*. Note that the use *of Val(txtAnswer)* in the test to get the numeric value out of the Variant data type.

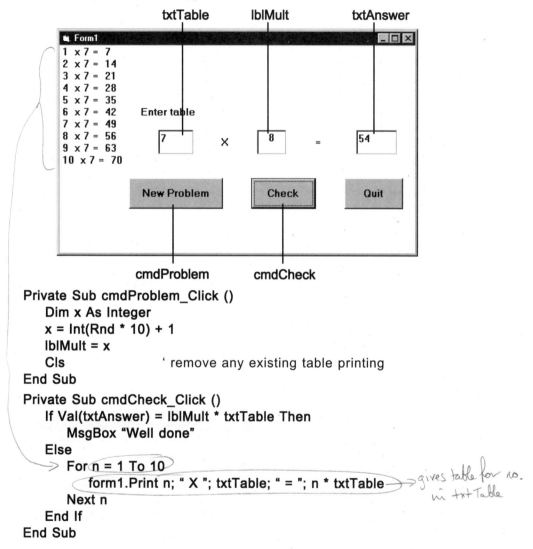

```
Private Sub cmdProblem_Click ()
    Dim x As Integer
    x = Int(Rnd * 10) + 1
    lblMult = x
    Cls                          ' remove any existing table printing
End Sub
Private Sub cmdCheck_Click ()
    If Val(txtAnswer) = lblMult * txtTable Then
        MsgBox "Well done"
    Else
        For n = 1 To 10
            form1.Print n; " X "; txtTable; " = "; n * txtTable
        Next n
    End If
End Sub
```

gives table for no.
in txtTable

Exercise 4

This takes the member's age into a Text Box named *txtAge*, and displays the results in the Labels *lblCategory* and *lblFees*. The calculations are done in code attached to the Button *cmdCheck*. The code could have been placed in the KeyPress procedure of the *txtAge* Text Box. Written there, it would have needed enclosing in an **If...End If** block so that it was only executed when the user pressed the [Enter] key.

```
If KeyAscii = 13 Then
    ...
```

```
Private Sub cmdCheck_Click()
Dim age As Integer
age = txtAge
Select Case age
    Case 0 To 16
        lblCategory = "Junior"
        lblFees = "£125"
    Case 17 To 54
        lblCategory = "Adult"
        lblFees = "£250"
    Case 55 To 80
        lblCategory = "Senior"
        lblFees = "£125"
    Case Else
        lblCategory = "Honorary"
        lblFees = "Free"

End Select
End Sub
```

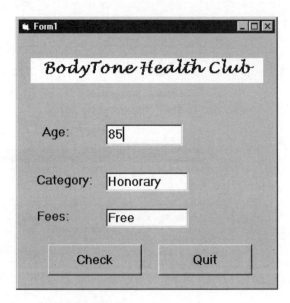

Chapter 5
Exercise 2

What you must remember here is the CheckBoxes act as toggle switches, so when a box is clicked, you must either turn the effect on or off. As these CheckBoxes set Font properties which are themselves toggles, there are two ways you can tackle this: either explicitly test the value of the CheckBox and set the Font property accordingly, or simply toggle the Font property when the corresponding CheckBox is clicked.

In these solutions, the CheckBoxes are named *chkBold*, *chkItalic* and *chkUnderline*, and the Text box is left as *Text1*.

The code for the first approach reads:

```
Private Sub chkBold_Click ()
    If chkBold Then
        Text1.FontBold = True
    Else
        Text1.FontBold = False
    End If
End Sub

Private Sub chkItalic_Click ()
    If chkItalic Then
        Text1.FontItalic = True
    Else
        Text1.FontItalic = False
    End If
End Sub
```

```
Private Sub chkUnderline_Click ()
    If chkUnderline Then
        Text1.FontUnderline = True
    Else
        Text1.FontUnderline = False
    End If
End Sub
```

The toggle approach uses the fact that FontBold, FontItalic and FontUnderline are Boolean values – they can only hold True or False. The statement:

```
FontBold = Not FontBold
```

will find the current value of the property, reverse it and assign it back to the property. That leads us to this much briefer code:

```
Private Sub chkBold_Click()
    Text1.FontBold = Not Text1.FontBold
End Sub

Private Sub chkItalic_Click()
    Text1.FontItalic = Not Text1.FontItalic
End Sub

Private Sub chkUnderline_Click()
    Text1.FontUnderline = Not Text1.FontUnderline
End Sub
```

Chapter 7

Exercise 1

This program works through the range of DrawModes (1 to 16), and crashes to a halt if the user tries to go beyond that. There are two buttons, *New Mode* and *Redraw*, and a label to display the current value. The *Redraw* button clears the form and draws a thick line of green in the corner of the form. The *New Mode* button moves to the next DrawMode, updates the label, and draws a thick line at right-angles to the other. Its colour, and what happens when it crosses the green line, varies with the DrawMode.

```
Private Sub Form_Load ()
    drawmode = 1
    label1 = drawmode
End Sub

Private Sub cmdNewMode_Click ()
    drawmode = drawmode + 1
    label1 = drawmode
    Line (100, 100)-(2000, 2000), QBColor(4)
End Sub

Private Sub cmdRedraw_Click ()
    Cls
    temp = drawmode
    drawmode = 13
    Line (100, 2000)-(2000, 100), QBColor(2)
    drawmode = temp
End Sub
```

Exercise 2

There are many alternative solutions here. One of the simplest is to place on the form three ScrollBars, with accompanying labels, and a Command button. The ScrollBars should be named *hsbRed*, *hsbGreen* and *hsbBlue*, and have their Max property set to 255. You will need a little code on their **Change** events to copy their values into the labels, so you can see what they are. The code on the button will combine the ScrollBar values into an RGB colour and pass this to a Circle or Line command, e.g.

```
Private Sub Draw_Click ()
    col = RGB(hsbRed, hsbGreen, hsbBlue)
    Circle (2000, 2000), 1000, col
End Sub
```

Exercise 3

This program draws concentric sets of circles in random colours at random places on the screen. But what it draws is less important than how the form is set up and how the code is activated. Notice the Properties settings for the form. The key ones are **BorderStyle = 0**, which turns off the border, and **WindowState = 2**, which sets it to full screen. The Properties could be set at design time, if preferred.

There are no controls on the form. The 'screensaver' code runs when the form is loaded.

```
Private Sub Form_Load()
    Dim x As Integer
    Dim y As Integer
    Dim Radius As Integer
    Dim colour As Long
    BackColor = &H0000000&          ' Black
    BorderStyle = 0                 ' None
    DrawMode = 13
    DrawStyle = 0
    DrawWidth = 1
    Form1.WindowState = 2           ' maximized
    Form1.Show
    Randomize
    Do
        x = Rnd(1) * (Width - 2000) ' new random number
        y = Rnd(1) * (Height - 2000)
        Radius = Rnd(1) * 4000 + 1000
        colour = QBColor(Rnd * 15)
        For ring = 1 To Radius Step 20  ' 0 step for solid circles
            Circle (x, y), ring, colour
            DoEvents
        Next ring
    Loop Until False ' i.e. forever
End Sub
```

The program is brought to a stop by either a mouse click or a keypress. All it takes is an End in each of the appropriate procedures. Ideally, MouseMove should also end the program, but the system will pick up the movement as you start the program and bring it to an instant halt. You might like to consider ways to get round this!

```
Private Sub Form_Click()
End
End Sub
Private Sub Form_KeyPress(KeyAscii As Integer)
End
End Sub
```

Chapter 8

Exercise 1

If you hit a snag here, it is probably in your choice of variable names. You cannot use *Width* as there is a statement with that name, and *Height* will give peculiar results because it will also refer to the Height property of the current control. Once you have found suitable names, the rest should be a piece of cake.

```
Function vol (ht As Single, wd As Single, ln As Single) As Single
    vol = ht * wd * ln
End Function
```

Exercise 2

The simplest solution here is to run backwards through the string, slicing off one letter at a time and adding them into a new string.

```
Function reverse (s As String) As String
    Dim temp As String
    temp = ""
    For n = Len(s) To 1 Step -1
        temp = temp & Mid(s, n, 1)
    Next n
    reverse = temp
End Function
```

Exercise 3

This can be developed directly from the *reverse* function. Just compare the reversed string with the original and if they match, assign 1 to *palindrome*.

```
Function palindrome (s As String) As Integer
    Dim temp As String
    temp = ""
    For n = Len(s) To 1 Step -1
        temp = temp & Mid(s, n, 1)
    Next n
    If temp = s Then palindrome = 1 Else palindrome = 0
End Function
```

Chapter 9

Exercise 1

If the new buttons are named *cmdDisplay*, *cmdEdit*, *cmdMinMax* and *cmdSort*, and if you are happy to run inputs through InputBoxes and outputs through MsgBoxes and print directly on the form, then the following code will meet the requirements:

```
Private Sub cmdDisplay_Click ()
    Form1.Cls
    Form1.Print "Item no.     Data "
    For n = 0 To 9
        Form1.Print n; "     "; dataset(n)
    Next n
End Sub

Private Sub cmdEdit_Click ()
    element = InputBox("Enter item number")
    dataset(element) = InputBox("New value for item " & element)
End Sub

Private Sub cmdMinMax_Click ()
    Dim Min As Single, Max As Single
    Min = dataset(0)                              ' starting values
    Max = dataset(0)
    For n = 1 To 9
        If dataset(n) < Min Then Min = dataset(n)   ' found smaller
        If dataset(n) > Max Then Max = dataset(n)  ' found larger
    Next n
    message = "The minimum value is " & Min
    message = message & Chr(10) & Chr(13)         ' new line
    message = message & "The maximum value is " & Max
    MsgBox message
End Sub

Private Sub cmdSort_Click ()                       ' simple bubble sort
    Dim temp As Single
    Dim sorted
    Do
        sorted = True
        For n = 0 To 8
            If dataset(n) > dataset(n + 1) Then
                temp = dataset(n)
                dataset(n) = dataset(n + 1)
                dataset(n + 1) = temp
                sorted = False
            End If
        Next n
    Loop Until sorted
    cmdDisplay_Click     ' force display routine
End Sub
```

Exercise 2

This was almost a trick question. That key line is the only line of code that is needed to change the text's colour:

```
Private Sub lblPalette_Click (Index As Integer)
    Text1.ForeColor = lblPalette(Index).BackColor
End Sub
```

Exercise 3

The most difficult part of this program is the code to scan the board for a winning line. I have set the board up as a Control array, using Text Boxes called *box*.

The New Game button (*cmdNew*) simply wipes the board and initialises the *status* variable, which will later hold the results of checking the lines..

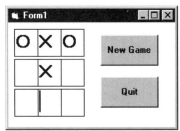

```
Private Sub cmdNew_Click()
    For n = 0 To 8
        box(n) = ""
    Next n
    status = 0
End Sub
```

The main block of code is in the *box*'s **Change** procedure, with the checking routine sliced off into a separate procedure called *checkboard*.

```
Private Sub Box_Change(Index As Integer)
    If Len(box(Index)) > 1 Then
        box(Index) = Left(box(Index), 1)      ' check only one letter
    End If
    box(Index) = UCase(box(Index))            ' capitalise it
    ' if used Ucase generates a Change - making this recursive
    ' the next line stops it finding an end game twice
    If status <> 0 Then Exit Sub
        If box(Index) = "X" Or box(Index) = "O" Then
            checkboard
            If status = 1 Then
            MsgBox "The Winner"
            Exit Sub
        End If
        If status = 2 Then MsgBox "It's a draw"
    End If
End Sub
```

The Boxes are arranged with the index numbers in this pattern:

```
0  1  2
3  4  5
6  7  8
```

The calculations in the code flow from that. To check the rows, we start from boxes 0, 3 and 6, and compare them with the boxes numbered +1 and +2. To check the columns, we start at 0, 1 and 2 and compare their contents with those numbered +3 and +6. For the diagonals, we need to check the two sets 0,4, 8 and 2, 4, 6.

The final check is for a full board, and that is just a matter of running through all the boxes to see if any are still empty. It's a crude system, and cannot spot the stalemates that can arise by move 7 or 8.

```
Private Sub checkboard()
    ' check rows
    For row = 0 To 6 Step 3
        If box(row) <> "" Then ' leftmost box X or O
```

```
            If box(row) = box(row + 1) And box(row) = box(row + 2) Then
                status = 1
                Exit Sub
            End If
        End If
    Next row
    ' check columns
    For col = 0 To 2
        If box(col) <> "" Then ' topmost box X or O
            If box(col) = box(col + 3) And box(col) = box(col + 6) Then
                status = 1
                Exit Sub
            End If
        End If
    Next col
    ' check diagonals
    If box(4) <> "" Then ' centre box X or O
        If box(0) = box(4) And box(0) = box(8) Then
            status = 1
            Exit Sub
        End If
        If box(2) = box(4) And box(2) = box(6) Then
            status = 1
            Exit Sub
        End If
    End If
    ' check for full board
    full = True
    For n = 0 To 8
        If box(n) = "" Then full = False
    Next n
    If full Then status = 2
End Sub
```

> The files for this program are available from the Visual Basic page at the author's Web site: http://www.tcp.co.uk/~macbride

Chapter 10
Exercise 1

There are many possible solutions here. This one makes a label, named *target*, appear at a random place on the form after a random delay. A timer counts out the random delay, and when it reaches the end, it makes the target visible and starts a second timer. Code on the **Click** event of the target picks up the count from the second timer, displays the result on a label, named *lblFeedback*, and sets the process off again by calling the *initialise* procedure.

The program shows something about the accuracy – or otherwise – of timing activities with Timers. In theory, you can set the Interval in milliseconds (1/1000ths of a second). In practice, an Interval of anything from 1 to 50, or even 100, will produce much the same result. The Visual Basic system has to monitor the keyboard, mouse and other aspects of the hardware, as well as keep an eye on any Timers, and it just can't get around to running them several hundred times a second. Set the Interval to 1000, and a Timer will tick away the seconds fairly accurately. Set it to 100, and it will be activated, pretty reliably, 10 times a second. That is the interval used for both Timers in this program.

```
general declarations
    Dim delay As Integer
    Dim counter As Integer
    Dim tenths As Long
Private Sub Form_Load ()
    Timer1.Interval = 100
    Timer2.Interval = 100
    initialise
End Sub
Sub initialise ()
    delay = Rnd * 10 + 1            ' initial delay before blob appears
    counter = 0
    tenths = 0
    Timer2.Enabled = False
    Timer1.Enabled = True
    lblTarget.Visible = False
    lblTarget.Top = Rnd * 5000      'random position
    lblTarget.Left = Rnd * 5000
End Sub
Private Sub lblTarget_Click ()
    lblTarget.Visible = False
    lblFeedback = "Response time = " & tenths / 10 & "Seconds"
    initialise
End Sub
Private Sub Timer1_Timer ()
    counter = counter + 1
    If counter = delay Then
    lblTarget.Visible = True
    Timer1.Enabled = False
    Timer2.Enabled = True
    End If
End Sub
Private Sub Timer2_Timer()
    tenths = tenths + 1
End Sub
```

> The files for this program are available from the Visual Basic page at the author's Web site:
> http://www.tcp.co.uk/~macbride

Exercise 2

Probably the best approach here is to have a Label (here called *lblCount*) that starts with a Caption of "10", and a Timer that has its Interval set to 1000 – giving one-second intervals. The code on the Timer should then read:

```
Sub Timer1_Timer ()
    lblCount = lblCount - 1
    If lblCount = 1 Then Timer1.Enabled = False
End Sub
```

Chapter 11
Exercise 5

The main problem here is in transferring the data from the file to the Caption of the options and the Question label, as you cannot Input into them. The solution is to take the data via a temporary variable, as we did with the Font properties. The right answer, which will be held in a variable, can be Input directly. This takes us to the following code, here attached to a button named *cmdNext*:

```
Sub cmdNext_Click ()
    If EOF(1) Then Exit Sub
    Input #1, temp
    lblQuestion = temp
    Input #1, temp
    Option1.Caption = temp
    Input #1, temp
    Option2.Caption = temp
    Input #1, temp
    Option3.Caption = temp
    Input #1, answer
    lblResult = ""
End Sub
```

Note, that for this to work, the file must have been opened already (as #1) – perhaps by the **Form_Load** procedure. For checking the answers, the simplest approach is to write "1","2" or "3", to match the correct Option number, into the file. The result can then be shown when the user clicks an Option. This code could end with a line to call up the next question, and update a variable to keep track of the score.

```
Sub Option1_Click ()
    If answer = "1" Then
        lblResult = "Correct"
    Else
        lblResult = "Wrong"
    End If
End Sub
```

A possible layout for a simple multi-choice test

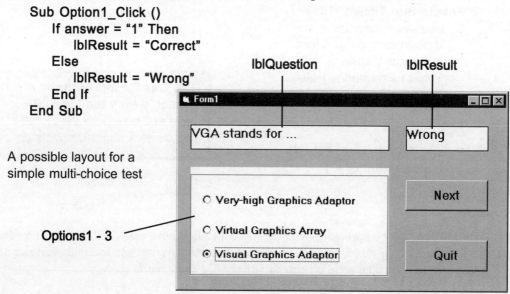

lblQuestion   lblResult

Options1 - 3

Appendix B: Controls summary

The **Name prefix** is the standard prefix that you should use when naming a control.

The **Main property** is the one that can be omitted when collecting a value from a control. For example, Text is the main property of a Text Box and the line *answer = Text1* has the same effect as *answer - Text1.Text*.

The **Default event** is the one that the code window will open onto when you first attach code to a control.

Those Properties marked with * are only available during runtime. The rest can be set at design time or during program execution.

Control	Name prefix	Main property	Default event
Check Box	chk	Value	Click
Combo Box	cbo	Text	Change
Command Button	cmd	Value*	Click
Directory List Box	dir	Path*	Change
Drive List Box	drv	Drive*	Change
File List Box	fil	FileName*	Change
Form	frm	N/A	Load
Frame	fra	Caption	DragDrop
Horizontal ScrollBar	hsb	Value	Change
Image	img	Picture	Click
Label	lbl	Caption	Click
List Box	lst	List(ListIndex)*	Click
Picture Box	pic	Picture	Click
Text Box	txt	Text	Change
Timer	tmr	Enabled	Timer
Vertical ScrollBar	hsb	Value	Change

Index

Index